AENEAS

Was he a hero?

Aeneas

VIRGIL'S EPIC RETOLD
FOR YOUNG READERS BY
EMILY FRENKEL
ILLUSTRATIONS BY
SIMON WELLER

Bristol Classical Press

This impression 2004
First published in 1986 by
Bristol Classical Press
an imprint of
Gerald Duckworth & Co. Ltd.
90-93 Cowcross Street, London EC1M 6BF
Tel: 020 7490 7300
Fax: 020 7490 0080
inquiries@duckworth-publishers.co.uk
www.ducknet.co.uk

A catalogue record for this book is available
from the British Library

ISBN 978-0-86292-198-9
EAN 9780862921989

Printed in Great Britain by
Biddles Ltd, King's Lynn, Norfolk

Contents

Virgil's own introduction:

"My poem is about war, and a man—
            a hero driven by Fate from Troy to Italy's shore.
He was tossed about on land and sea by the forces
                                                of heaven,
        stirred by the unforgiving, savage anger
                of the goddess Juno,
                and he suffered much in war,
till at last he could found a city
                and bring his gods into Latium.
From this came
                the Latin race,
                        the elders of Alba,
                                and the walls of lofty Rome.

Goddess of poets, remind me, tell me the cause of it all:
                how was her power insulted?
What hurt, what grief could drive the queen of the gods
to plan such ordeals for a man known to be true,
and force him to suffer so much?
                Are the heavenly gods so spiteful?"

Foreword

THIS story is based on a famous poem called the *Aeneid*, written in Latin by the Roman poet, Virgil, about two thousand years ago. It relates the adventures of the hero, Aeneas, a man "driven by Fate", who escaped from the burning ruins of Troy and led his people to a new home in a distant land.

A re-telling like this introduces the story to the modern reader who is not yet familiar with Roman mythology or the grand poetic style of ancient epic. Descriptions and dialogue have been improvised — storytellers, ancient and modern, claim this licence — but the sequence of events and general atmosphere are presented as in Virgil's poem.

I hope that readers who enjoy this book will want to read the *Aeneid* in its original form. The English translation by C. Day Lewis is a vivid rendering in forceful modern verse. The best way, however, to enjoy the brilliance of the *Aeneid* is to study Latin, and read the very words Virgil himself wrote.

I should like to express my thanks to the pupils of Ascham School, Sydney, who heard this story told and said it was 'exciting but terribly sad', and to Mrs Maureen Brooke, who typed the manuscript.

Prologue   The Judgement of Paris

LONG, long ago, there was a rich and splendid city called Troy. Surrounded by high walls like a fortress, it commanded a great stretch of the country known to us as Turkey, and was famous throughout the ancient world for its wealth and power.

Old King Priam was its ruler. He and his Queen, Hecuba, had many children, but among them was one who was fated to destroy them all.

The warning came even before the child was born. Queen Hecuba dreamt that she had given birth, not to a human child, but to a blazing torch, a firebrand. In a terrifying instant she saw the flames leaping over the whole city of Troy. She awoke, screaming, to a safe, calm world, and gave birth to a healthy boy. They called him Paris.

Paris was a remarkably pretty baby, but his elder sister, Cassandra, shrieked when she saw him and flung herself savagely on his tiny body. "Kill him!" she cried. "He will burn down all of Troy! Kill him, before he murders us!"

Everyone knew about Cassandra, but no one spoke of her much, except in whispers. Some said the god Apollo had robbed her of her wits. Everyone pitied her, soothed her rages, and ignored her words.

This time, however, Hecuba could not dismiss her

1

daughter's fearful warning, for she remembered her own. nightmare of the fiery torch. She spoke urgently to King Priam.

"We must know the will of the gods. Let us consult the oracle, my lord."

The message was sent. Queen Hecuba waited, knowing the answer in her heart.

"The oracle advises you to expose this child without delay. He must die, abandoned on the mountainside, or he will bring death to Troy."

The baby was bundled up at once, and a servant was instructed to leave him in the woods. But when the man came back a few days later to see what had happened to the child, he found Paris alive and happy, being licked and nuzzled by a family of bear cubs.

"The gods want this child to live," thought the servant; and he took Paris home to his wife.

So Paris grew up as a humble country lad, and became a handsome youth, popular among his fellow villagers. His daily task was to mind sheep and goats on the hillsides, and his greatest pleasure was playing his shepherd's pipe. He never gave a thought to the royal house of Troy.

On one such carefree day a strange young man appeared – from nowhere – and declared that he was Mercury, the messenger of the immortal gods. Paris believed him: his skin shone silver, his shoes and cap were winged, and a living snake twisted about his staff.

"By the will of almighty Jupiter, king of gods and men, lord of thunder and lightning, you must judge the fairest of three goddesses and settle the quarrel that disturbs the peace of Olympus, home of the gods."

Paris had no time to collect his thoughts. Somewhere

behind him, a female voice proclaimed loudly, "Of course, the prize is mine. I am Juno, the Queen of the gods!"

"No! I am the loveliest by far!" said a second, softer voice.

"You are just empty-headed, Venus," a third retorted, in deeper tones. "No one could call you fair."

Paris spun round. Three ladies, all astonishingly beautiful, hovered just above the grass before him. The sheep were huddled in frozen panic by the stream.

"Choose me, Paris," said royal Juno, "and I will make you king of a mighty empire."

"Choose me," said grave Minerva, "and I will make you the wisest man on earth."

"Choose me," Venus only murmured, "and I will give you the loveliest woman in the world to be your wife."

Paris did not hesitate. He told himself later that the bribe had nothing to do with it; Venus was, in any case, the most beautiful goddess of all.

So Paris won the loveliest woman in the world. Unfortunately she was already the wife of another man. Her name was Helen, and her husband was Menelaus, King of the city of Sparta, far away in Greece.

Paris did not remain a shepherd for long. An athletic contest was held in Troy, and Paris, like hundreds of other young men, went up to the city to take part. His looks and his skill at sports would have attracted attention in any gathering, and no one was surprised when he was selected for presentation to the King and Queen. Shy and conscious of his rough clothes, he was led into the royal presence.

"Ah, the young man from . . . ," Priam began. Someone rushed through the crowd, flung herself on Paris, and scratched his face, howling, "Kill him! Kill him! He brings death to Troy!"

Embarrassed servants pulled Cassandra away. King Priam fussed around the astonished youth, wiping the blood from his cheeks, repeating explanations and apologies. The Queen sat very still. But when the commotion was over she rose and approached the young man. Calmly, with resignation, she kissed him. "You are my son, Paris," she said in a clear voice for all to hear. "The gods have willed that you should live. Welcome home."

So Paris was restored to the royal house. He did not take long to learn the ways of princes, though his elder brother Hector found him too gentle for the warlike arts of sword and spear. He took his share of royal duties, entertaining foreign visitors and hearing embassies from overseas.

The day came when he sailed to Greece, to visit Menelaus, King of Sparta, in a royal party which included his cousin, Aeneas, and many other high-born Trojans. Menelaus and his Queen, Helen, welcomed them with splendid hospitality.

A few days after the arrival of the Trojan embassy, Menelaus was called away to Crete, where his grandfather had died. When he returned home, the Trojans had gone, taking with them much treasure, and Helen, Queen of Sparta.

Menelaus was beside himself with fury and hurt pride. He went at once to his brother, Agamemnon, the mighty King of Mycenae. Together they sent messages to the kings of every city in Greece, urging them to gather their armies and prepare for a great war against Troy.

The war raged for ten years. It ended with Troy sacked and in flames, Priam, Hector and Paris dead, and Hecuba and her daughters dragged off to miserable slavery.

A small group of survivors, led by Aeneas, whose mother happened to be the goddess Venus, escaped from the burning city. This book tells the story of their adventures.

'Paris + Venus
parents
to
aeneas

I   Aeneas is Shipwrecked at Carthage

FROM high Olympus, hidden from the earth by cloud and mist, Juno was watching a line of ships creeping towards the coast of Italy. Tiny they looked, frail as insects, but Juno, Queen of the gods, raged in helpless fury, because these distant, fragile ships were stronger than all her hatred.

They were the ships from Troy. For seven years now they had been making their voyage, groping from one strange, unfriendly coast to another, in search of a new home. Troy was gone, burnt to the ground. Already weeds were beginning to cover its blackened ruins.

Troy was gone, but the Trojan race still clung to life, and Juno could not crush it. She hated these mortals with that bitter, brooding grudge that grows from injured pride, increasing all the more because it can never win.

She could never forget the judgement of Paris. Paris, son of old King Priam of Troy, had dared to overlook the queenly charms of Juno, and award the title of Most Beautiful to Venus, the goddess no man could resist. Juno had felt the insult deep within her. She vowed to punish Paris and all his Trojan race.

With glee she had watched the Greeks burn Troy, and take back the woman Paris had stolen. With relish she had

7

followed the Trojan survivors as they suffered a cruel voyage. But she could not enjoy the final triumph, the complete destruction of the people she hated. The Trojans were in the hand of Fate, and Fate was stronger than all the gods. So Juno nursed her anger, and waited.

To make matters worse, the survivors were led by Aeneas, the mortal son of that shameless creature, Venus herself. She had taken the Trojan Anchises as her lover, binding herself even more closely to the nation of Paris. Juno could see Aeneas, the son of Venus and Anchises, standing on the prow of the Trojan flagship, scanning the horizon for the first glimpse of his promised land.

She knew what Fate had decreed. This Aeneas would found a new settlement. Its people would grow great, a race mightier than Troy had ever been, rulers of the world. One day they would come to Carthage, Juno's own favourite city, and ravage it as cruelly as the Greeks had ravaged Troy. Juno could not prevent them.

Nevertheless she could try. Using the mysterious paths known only to the gods, she made her way to a faraway cave, the secret dwelling of the Wind-King.

"Mighty King of the Winds," Juno began, charming that lonely ruler with soft words and sweet smiles, although he could scarcely hear her above the howling and whistling of his turbulent subjects, "do one favour for me, and I shall reward you well. Some people I detest — never mind why — are sailing near the coast of Italy. Stir up your winds and order them to rouse a frightful storm, enough to wreck those ships and drown every man. I promise to give you any handmaid of mine you choose to be your bride."

The King's shadowed eyes gleamed for an instant, and the winds whirled away at his command.

Aboard the Trojan ships, there was no time for panic. Sails were ripped from their masts; the decks were a riot of rigging, timber, torn wineskins belching their contents, all mingled with sea-water and blood. There was a tearing and slapping of wet fabric, and the scream and crack of wood bent beyond the limit of its strength. The low, desperate babble of human confusion was broken now and then by the shriek of some poor creature crushed by a mast, or the shrill neighing of a horse swept overboard into the boiling sea.

Human wits and muscles could do nothing. Aeneas, his legs gripping a rocking ladder, raised his hands to the sky. "Why didn't we die in Troy?" he cried, but the words of his prayer were lost in the gale; the whole ship seemed to be wailing the same lament.

In the depths of the sea, the god Neptune was disturbed. Someone was tampering with his watery kingdom. At once he rose to the surface, exclaimed angrily at the scene, and stretched his calming trident over the waves. "Go back, you winds! Tell your king to rule his own domain. Leave me to mine!"

Over the smooth water seven of the Trojan ships limped to a nearby coast. Land, any land, was blessing enough — for the time being. The survivors, too exhausted to be happy at their good luck, too dazed to notice that thirteen ships were missing, lay almost lifeless on the sand.

Aeneas was the first to recover himself, but there was no joy or relief in his thoughts. "Again and again the gods make fun of us. Do they mean to starve us this time or have us butchered by savages? At least in Troy I could have had a hero's death." The memory of Troy brought back other sorrows, and Aeneas wept for his wife, lost in the burning city, for his aged father, dead in Sicily, their last port of call, and for his little son, Iulus, probably drowned at sea.

All around him now people were stirring. As each saw how ragged and hopeless the others looked, and how desolate and strange was the land, a despairing silence came over the whole band. No one asked where the missing ships were, but all of them turned their eyes to Aeneas.

Somehow he managed to overcome his own despair: "Come on, everyone! Start collecting wood! Achates, how about a fire? Lend me your bow and arrows — I'm going to climb that rock to see if there's any game I can shoot for our dinner." Gratefully they obeyed him. Obviously, with Aeneas in such a confident mood, there was nothing to worry about.

One person, however, fully understood and shared the fear Aeneas was hiding from his men. High in the dwelling-place of the gods, his mother Venus was pleading with almighty Jupiter.

"Father, how can you let this happen? You promised a great future for my son Aeneas. Well, there he lies, cast away on an unfriendly shore, most of his ships missing, and all because of the spite of a certain goddess. Father, have you forgotten how he worships you and all the gods?"

Jupiter turned his far-seeing eyes away from the world of men, and smiled at his daughter's tears.

"Don't worry, my dear. Juno likes to stir up trouble, but there is nothing she can really change. I have seen the Fates and heard their decree. Your Aeneas will go on to found a great nation, the mightiest and most noble the mortal world has ever known. His home will be in the land of Italy, where he will fight heroic battles and win for himself a kingdom and a royal bride. In years to come, his descendant — a youth called Romulus — will build a city and call it Rome. Even Juno will change her mind, and with the help of all the gods, the people of Rome will rule over all the world, including those Greeks who think they have put an end to Troy. They will have a mighty leader who will be called Caesar."

On the beach, Aeneas' men had eaten well. Their clothes had dried by the heat of the reassuring fire, and they looked forward to sleep. Aeneas stretched himself out to lie alongside them, but there was to be no easy rest for him. Over and over, the same questions tormented him: "What has happened to Iulus? Where are we? How long can we be safe from attack? It's nearly winter — even if we can manage to repair our ships, will the weather let us sail?"

At first light Aeneas left his slumbering crew. He began to walk away from the sea, restlessly and with no clear purpose; but he was glad to be joined by his friend, Achates. They walked quickly, in silence, alert for any surprise attack.

There was a sudden rustling. Instantly they gripped their spears and stood ready, Aeneas a little in front. There was a moment's pause, and then from the thicket stepped a beautiful young girl, dressed in a hunting outfit, and carrying two spears. She seemed unafraid: "Have you seen one of my sisters anywhere? She's dressed like me."

"No!" Aeneas heard his voice, sharp with relief. "No. We haven't seen anyone. But please, before you go, tell us what this place is called. We are sailors, shipwrecked on this coast. We have no idea where we are."

The girl did not seem surprised at all, and smiled. "You needn't be afraid. No one will harm you here. This is the coast of Africa, a land full of barbaric tribes, but the kingdom hereabouts belongs to civilised people, settlers from Tyre. We are building a new city, called Carthage. Our leader is Queen Dido."

"A woman!" Achates exclaimed. "In such a barbaric and dangerous land!"

"She is no ordinary woman, as you will see. Her brother Pygmalion was ruler in Tyre — the worst sort of tyrant. He secretly murdered Dido's husband, in cold blood, by the family altar, and seized all their wealth. But the story goes that her husband's ghost warned Dido to escape. She packed her possessions, organized her friends, and sailed many miles to this coast. Here she outwitted the tribal chiefs and tricked them into selling her a good plot of ground, enough to build a fine city. Many of the chiefs have asked for her hand in marriage, overcome by her beauty and wisdom, but she has sworn to remain true to her husband's memory. But now, you must tell me who you are."

Aeneas sighed, and began. "Our story has no happy ending. We are from Troy, a noble city, where King Priam once ruled a splendid empire. Perhaps you have heard of it? If you have, you would know that it is gone for ever, burnt to the ground by the Greeks. My name is Aeneas, of the royal house of Troy. People call me Aeneas the True, because I carried away from my burning home my aged father, and the statues of my household gods. We are — or rather, we were — making for a western land, called Italy, to found a new city. I had twenty ships under my command. We were in sight of Italy, a few hours would have brought us there, when some malevolent god sent a terrible storm to destroy us. Thirteen of our ships are missing; the rest lie shattered on the beach. We have no hope of completing our voyage."

The girl had been listening with friendly sympathy, but now her manner became abrupt. "Nonsense! Your ships are quite safe! . . . Don't stare at me like that. I have some knowledge of signs from heaven. I suggest you go up to our city. I am sure the Queen will help you." She turned away, and as she did so, her figure seemed to become taller and more graceful and her hair shone about her head. Achates caught his breath at the miracle, but Aeneas only hid his face in his hands. "Mother," he cried, "why trick me like this? Why not speak to me openly, face to face?" But Venus was gone, with one parting gesture that swept a thick mist around Aeneas and his friend, making them invisible to human eyes.

The new city was a hive of industry. Everywhere buildings were being erected; workmen were clearing plots of ground, lifting blocks of stone, and chiselling fine sculptures. A noise of hammering and sawing filled the air. The Trojans gazed up at the walls already towering above them. Aeneas imagined such a city being built for his weary Trojans, and envied these refugees who had found a new home.

Most splendid of all was a huge temple, everywhere plated with shining bronze. It was Dido's special tribute to her guardian goddess, Juno. Aeneas ran his eyes over a frieze, carved in rich detail on the doors. He suddenly realized what it depicted: "Achates, look! It's our war! See, that must be Troy. And here's old Priam, and Hector, and our chariots! Oh, look here, that monster Achilles dragging Hector's body . . ." Aeneas wept for his city and his friends, and wept to think that their sufferings were known even in this remote land.

Trumpets blasted, and there was a rush of excited citizens into the temple courtyard. Aeneas and Achates, invisible in their cloak of mist, watched in wonder as a procession of officials took up their positions. They were followed by other attendants in gold and purple robes, and slaves bearing a magnificent throne set on a high platform. Another trumpet-blast announced the arrival of the Queen. Dido appeared, royal not only in dress and bearing; she had all the radiant majesty of a goddess.

Aeneas had met many royal ladies in Troy. Hecuba had been a dignified and well-respected Queen, and her daughters had all been striking princesses much courted by young noblemen. No one in Troy had ever pretended, however, that they did much more than bring grace and gentleness into a world ruled and managed by men.

But here was Dido, judging and settling disputes, pronouncing in a sweet, firm voice verdicts which were instantly obeyed. Aeneas was struck with wonder and admiration. He was considering how best to approach such an unusual ruler, when a commotion amongst the crowd attracted his attention.

Officials were rapping out commands to a group of new arrivals, dirty miserable-looking wretches who were pushed before the throne. "Who are these men?" Dido demanded.

"Foreigners, your majesty. We thought it best to bring them to you at once."

"Of course. Who will speak for you, strangers?"

"I will!"

Aeneas, hardly believing it, recognised the voice of one

of his missing captains, Ilioneus: "Your gracious majesty, we are homeless refugees from Troy, sailing to a western land called Italy to found a new city. A storm drove us to your shores, where your guards arrested us and threatened to burn our ships. Stop them, we beg you! We are not criminals or pirates. Our leader was Aeneas, a noble prince, famous for his loyalty to the gods and his country, and a mighty warrior in battle. He must have perished in the storm. If you will help us, your majesty, we may still reach Italy, if that is the gods' will. If not, we could return to Sicily, where we have friends to welcome us. We are in your hands."

Ilioneus bowed, and the other Trojans murmured in agreement. Dido did not hesitate, but rose and signed to the guards to release them. "Have no fear, my friends. I know exactly how you feel. I, too, have been a refugee. We have all heard of Troy, and of the courage of your people, and of your great leader, Aeneas. I will give you all the help you need. If you decide to sail, I will make sure your ships are repaired, and send you under escort to Italy, or Sicily, or wherever you like. If you prefer to stay here, you may live freely in Carthage and share our city. I will give orders for a search to be made for Aeneas. Perhaps he is still alive, lost somewhere on the shores of our kingdom."

This was too much for Aeneas and Achates. They rushed forward, and their cloak of mist melted away. With an invisible hand, the goddess Venus poured vigour and grace over Aeneas, so that he stepped out of the crowd, tall and straight, with shining hair and eyes, and the fresh, untroubled features of a god. "I am here − Aeneas of Troy! Madam, you have given us back our hopes. If ever we can, we will repay you for your kindness, but even if we can never do so, may the gods bless you and all your people for the way you have received us!"

The next moment there was eager hand-shaking and delighted questioning and cries of relief and joy. Dido, astonished at first, laughed with pleasure at the happy scene of reunion, and the people of Carthage, too, caught the mood and broke out in cheers and applause.

"Sir," Dido said at last, extending her hand, "I am delighted to see you safe. My kingdom is at your disposal. Please make yourself at home. I should be honoured if you would join me at dinner tonight. We have heard many tales of Troy and of your valiant deeds, Aeneas. I am most anxious to hear them from your own lips. All of you are welcome, gentlemen."

Aeneas found himself being escorted into the temple, where Dido offered prayers of thanksgiving to the gods. Down by the ships, the sailors were amazed by the immediate delivery of every kind of food, abundant wine from the royal cellars, and clothing to outfit the whole crew like princes.

Aeneas could not wait to see his little son. He sent Achates to bring the boy at once to Dido's palace, together with some gifts of jewellery and silks rescued from the ruins of Troy and luckily saved in the shipwreck.

Venus had been watching these developments from afar, partly content, partly fearful. She knew that Carthage was a city dedicated to Juno. How long would it be before Dido's hospitality wore thin, and Juno caused her to plot some cruel end for Aeneas? It would be safer to bind Dido more closely to Aeneas. So Venus called to her other son, the little god of Love.

"Come, Cupid," she said, "I have a very important task for you. You are just about the same size as my little grandson, Iulus. I want you to take his place at Dido's banquet tonight. As soon as you get the chance, you must pierce her heart with one of your magic arrows, so that she can think of nothing else but a desperate love for Aeneas."

Venus waited for the right moment; she plucked Iulus up, and carried him, wrapped in gentle sleep, to a secret and beautiful place far away. Achates escorted Cupid, now looking exactly like the young prince, to Dido's palace, along with the gifts Aeneas had requested.

"So this is your son, Aeneas. What a handsome boy, with the makings of a noble warrior. You said his name was Iulus?" Dido lifted the child on to her knee.

"That is his name, though at home we often called him Ascanius. Give the Queen a kiss, son. We owe our lives to her."

The feast began. Servants handed the guests garlands for their heads, and scented water to wash their hands. Sweet music played, and course after course was carried in, displayed on platters of exquisite design. Aeneas and his officers savoured every morsel of the food set before them, eagerly drank the rich wine, and began to forget the years of hardship and sorrow.

Dido sat with the child on her knee, and found herself more and more entranced by the sight of Aeneas. The image of her late husband, which had haunted her thoughts day and night, began to blur and fade. Again and again, she called for a toast, her conversation sparkled with wit, and she applauded the musicians heartily and often. Courtiers began to remark under their breath that the Queen looked particularly bright and happy tonight.

The hour grew late, but still Dido talked, asking how Priam and Hector had died, wanting to know every detail of Achilles' chariot, every feature of Helen's beauty: "Speak, Aeneas. I want to know it all from the very beginning. Tell us what happened, from the day you left Troy. Leave nothing out. I must hear every one of your adventures, every single moment of your marvellous story. Come, begin."

For Monday

II The Last Hours of Troy

THE conversation died away. All the company turned to Aeneas.

"Madam, you cannot realise how grim my story is. It's late — perhaps your guests would prefer to hear it some other time?" But the Carthaginian nobles were keen to listen, and the Queen insisted.

"Well, if you are all so eager, I must begin the tale. As you know, the Greeks made a cruel attack on the city of Troy with one thousand ships and all the men they could raise. Their reason, they said, was just: to recover Helen, a shameless woman who happened to prefer our prince Paris to her weak-minded husband, Menelaus of Sparta. At the time, our sense of honour made us ready to fight for Helen — her name sticks in my throat now — and we seemed better off than the Greeks, since we had strong walls and friendly country all around. The gods kept their will hidden from us then.

For ten years, we stood up to their siege. Our Crown Prince, Hector, the finest man in Troy, fell at the hand of Achilles. Even Paris, whose talents were more suited to love than fighting, died like a soldier. But don't think the

21

losses were all on our side. When the dreaded Achilles met his fate, we cheered at the news.

Every day we would rise at dawn and peer over our walls at the Greek camp, wondering whose turn it was that day to win, and whose to die. So can you imagine how we felt when one morning we saw the beach deserted and all the enemy ships gone?

For the first time in ten years we could walk freely on our own soil outside the city walls. We were cautious at first, suspecting a trap, but soon we flung open the gates and surged out in crowds to enjoy the clean, fresh space. A city during a long siege is not too pleasant. We ran about in aimless delight, many of us with grown children who, after ten years' siege, had never yet stepped outside the gates. We thronged the Greek camping ground, gaily pointing out to our sons the meeting-place of the enemy kings; we made jokes about Agamemnon and Ajax and crafty Ulysses. AkA Odypseus　　Menelaus Bro　another Gr. leader,

You may think it incredible, but we were so absorbed in our good fortune that it was some time before anyone noticed that the beach was not entirely empty. Some distance from the silent camping-ground stood a massive wooden construction. It was in the likeness of an enormous horse. We gathered round, puzzled, and a little fearful. It cast a dark shadow on us. We stared up at its open eye-slits, and, for a while, no one knew what to say.

Then people started to have ideas. Some said it was a tribute from the enemy, who must have learned to respect us. Others thought it was a sacred image which should be placed in our city to bring us luck. Still others insisted it was a trap. The crowd was buzzing with excited talk, when a priest of Neptune, Laocoon by name, came racing angrily down from the city and forced his way into our midst. 'Burn the horse! You mustn't trust it, people of Troy!' he roared. 'Never mind what it is. I dread the Greeks no less when I see them offering gifts!' Saying this, like a madman, Laocoon flung a spear at the horse's belly. It stuck there, quivering, and we held our breath, waiting for a sign from heaven.

The sound of a scuffle made us look round. We forgot Laocoon. Some of our soldiers had arrested a man in Greek dress, and were dragging him before King Priam. Here, we thought, was a way to get to the truth. The fellow took a good look at all of us, and then, stretching out his manacled hands to Priam, begged us to spare his life.

'My name is Sinon,' he said. 'I am a Greek — I don't deny it. Before you kill me — for I know you mean to do so — hear my wretched story. It won't take long. I first joined the army as a squire to Palamedes, a noble and worthy officer. If you have heard of him, you will know that he was against this war, and that he suffered cruelly from the plots of that slippery villain, Ulysses.

'Once my master was dead, I myself became the butt of Ulysses' malice. He worked to turn the minds of the others against me, and at last his great opportunity came. Our prophet Calchas declared that we would never make a safe return to Greece unless the gods received a sacrifice of human blood. He took his time. He didn't name me straight away. He waited for rumour to do its work. No one protested when I was seized, bound and garlanded like a sacrificial beast, and led to the holy place for slaughter. Well, a chance came, and I took it. I escaped to the marsh and hid there all night. When I dared to come out, the Greeks were gone.

'So now I have no country and no home. I can never
return to Greece. And I can expect no mercy from you
Trojans, for naturally you hate every Greek on earth.'

He sounded so pitiful that we forgot our hatred of
anyone Greek. King Priam spoke for us all: 'Have no fear,
friend. You may stay safe with us. Why should we spoil
such a happy day? Untie his bonds. But tell us just one
thing; what is the purpose of this huge horse? Do you
know?'

Sinon rubbed at his wrists, and stretched his hands to the
sky before he spoke: 'All you gods of heaven and earth and
of the lower world, witness the truth of my words! There
can be no sin now in telling the secrets of the Greeks. You
may know, great King, that for some time now the Greeks
have suffered the ill-will of the goddess Minerva. That's
why they have gone back to Greece to renew their luck, to
return with good omens and finish the war with the gods on
their side. This horse they built as an offering to Minerva,
so big that you could not possibly get it through your gates.
They planned that if you harmed the horse, Minerva's
anger would fall upon you. If you could take it inside your
city, of course, then its luck would favour you instead of
the Greeks.'

His words had already made up our minds, but something else happened, so horrible and unearthly that I must
force myself to describe it to you.

From the sea there came suddenly two enormous snakes,
with ghastly, blood-red crests and immense coils that
seemed to swallow up the waves. We watched, helpless, as
they neared the shore, slid over dry land with the same
relentless motion, and headed straight for us. We could
see their forked tongues darting from their fearsome jaws.

The priest Laocoon, standing near the shore with his two sons, was just beginning a sacred ritual. Our cries of warning were frozen in our throats: the monsters wrapped their dreadful forms about the three of them. Limbs were swallowed in a murderous embrace. In an instant all were gone, and the serpents slid away into Minerva's temple.

Obviously, we thought, Laocoon had been punished for his insult to the sacred horse. We decked it with garlands and flowers, our children joined hands to sing and dance around it, and with ropes and rollers we hauled it to the walls. As Sinon had said, the gates were too narrow: at once we tore down part of the walls we no longer needed and brought the huge trophy into the centre of Troy. Cassandra, Priam's crazy daughter, screamed a warning of doom, but, as usual, no one took any notice of her.

That night we feasted. That night was the happiest in ten years. That night, we could sleep. We could not know that the Greek fleet was sailing back to our shores, or that Sinon was opening the belly of the great horse to let out thirty picked Greek warriors who had been hidden inside all the time. We slept on, while he guided them through our streets.

To me, there came a warning; in a dream I saw Hector, our noblest hero, his face grimy and his hair matted with blood and filth. For the moment I forgot that he was dead, butchered long ago by Achilles, and I called out to him, 'What has happened, Hector? Where have you been all this time? How do you come to be in such a pitiful state?'

He did not answer me directly: 'Go, Aeneas!' he cried, 'Don't stay here. Troy is lost. The Greeks have broken in. Don't try to fight them. Even I, great Hector, failed to drive them back. Save yourself, and the gods of our home! Escape to a new land across the seas.'

Startled and horrified, I reached towards him, but the figure faded and vanished. I ran to the porch. In every direction was flame. I stood transfixed. My neighbour's house crumbled into a glowing whirlwind of grit and smoke. I became aware of the commotion of running footsteps and screams that tore at my very nerves.

Now I moved quickly. I seized my weapons. I was no stranger to fighting, but never before had I been driven by such blind, heedless fury to rush out and kill, kill any Greeks I found, and drown my rage in their blood.

I met a friend, Panthus, leading his small grandson by the hand. 'No use, Aeneas!' he called, 'Troy is finished!' But I ignored him and rallied all those who would still fight. There were plenty of good, stout-hearted fellows who would not shrink from death, among them one Coroebus, who was engaged to the princess Cassandra.

At first we did well. We cut down a party of Greeks, and put on their armour as a disguise. Then, mingling with the enemy in the dark, we killed quite a number, while others ran in terror for their ships or hid in the Horse's belly. Poor Coroebus fell in a mad attempt to save Cassandra, when he saw her, eyes wild and hair flying, dragged off by the brawny lout, Ajax of Locris.

We forced our way to the citadel, the high fortress of old Troy, where the defenders were tearing up sections of the battlements and hurling them down on the heads of the Greeks. Here our disguise betrayed us; we found ourselves attacked from above by our own friends. My men were swept away; I, alone, slipped into the fortress by a back door.

I was now in the halls of King Priam's palace, once the home of a peaceful and prosperous court. After running from room to deserted room, I reached the inner court-yard. This place was open to the sky, dominated by a splendid tree which spread its branches protectively over an altar to the city's gods. Huddled about its great roots, like terrified birds, were Queen Hecuba and her daughters. The old King stood before them, absurdly dressed in the armour of his youth, which fitted loosely about his stooped and shrunken shoulders.

'Don't be silly, my love,' I heard the Queen coax, in a voice firm but resigned, 'Come, sit here with us. The gods will protect us. You're no match for young Pyrrhus.' But the old man fixed his eyes on the main door and, with a trembling right arm, raised his spear.

A gasping figure lurched through the doorway. I recog-nized Priam's youngest son, Polites. He was completely spent, sobbing for breath, and could only grope for the arms that stretched to him from the altar. A wound gaped in his back. Behind him gloated the dazzling form of Pyrrhus, son of Achilles.

Pyrrhus laughed to see the youth stumble towards his mother, slip, and die before her eyes. Then he turned his attention to the frail old man straining to balance the heavy spear, and stood, hands on hips, braying with hideous amusement. Priam made one effort, and the spear clat-tered feebly on the paving-stones at his feet.

'Monster!' cried the King. 'Even your father Achilles was a gentleman, compared with you. He treated me decently once, and gave me back Hector's body when I asked him. He did not amuse himself by murdering boys in front of their mothers.'

Pyrrhus laughed more loudly than ever, and then strode towards the King, and seized him by his thin white hair: 'So you knew my father; you can give him my regards when you meet him in the underworld. Be sure you let him know how soft and gentle I've become,' and, there, before the holy altar, he butchered noble Priam, King of Troy.

I did not wait any more. Priam reminded me of something I should have remembered before everything else: my own old, crippled father, my dear wife, Creusa, and my helpless little boy. You would think no power on earth could have made me stop then, as I sped through halls and passages. But suddenly I stood quite still when I saw *her*, skulking alone at the foot of an altar − Helen. Her beauty was still unmatched. Like a goddess, she was ever young and flawless.

I drew my sword and advanced on her. Now she would pay for the suffering she had caused to Greeks and Trojans alike. She had abandoned home and husband for a wild affair with Paris, the least heroic of all the sons of Priam. I would show her there was one Trojan she could not charm.

I can remember her eyes, pleading but somehow not cowardly. I remember that her skin seemed even lovelier because it was taut and pale. But I would have killed her all the same, if my goddess-mother had not appeared and plucked away my sword.

Venus reminded me of my real duty. 'Hurry, my son. Your family needs you. Waste no more time in killing. Look, I will open your eyes to the truth. See how the city is ringed by hostile gods. Neptune is shaking the foundations. Juno is leading the Greek troops herself, and there is Minerva, with the terrible Gorgon on her shield, roaring the battle-cry. Save your own family, Aeneas! There is very little time left.'

Nothing could delay me now. In a moment I was inside the familiar rooms, with my son clutching at my knees, and Creusa's arms around my neck. 'It's all right,' I kept saying, 'We're leaving at once, all of us. We must trust the gods.'

I had not taken account of my father's stubborn will: 'Here I was born, and here I stay!' he thundered, 'No one is dragging me round the world at my age. If I die, I die — in my own house!'

I tried pleas, arguments, force — all useless. Leaving him to the Greeks was unthinkable. He was crippled and could not even stand to arms for a warrior's death. Only a sign from the gods, he said, would change his mind.

No sooner had he spoken, than the miracle occurred. Flames began to flicker over Iulus' head. Before we could even recover our senses, our terror had turned to amazement. For the child was quite unharmed, and smiled happily at us, while all round his hair shone a blazing ring of fire.

My father broke the silence: 'This is a sign. Let us bow to the will of heaven. Lead on, Aeneas, wherever the gods guide you.' And as he spoke there was a crash of thunder, and a comet streaked across the sky.

In relief I gasped out instructions to the servants to make their way, by separate routes, to a temple of Ceres near the city gates. All the time I was speaking, I was gathering a few possessions, and tying a lionskin about my shoulders. I signed to someone to fetch out the home-gods, and I handed the precious images to my father.

'Hold them tightly, sir!' I said, 'We have a long way to

go!' With a strange gladness I stooped and lifted the old man on to my shoulders. 'Come here, Ascanius,' I called to the child, using his pet-name, 'hold your father's hand. Creusa, stay close.' So we started on our way.

For many frantic hours, I had been roaming boldly about the stricken city. I had stormed through bands of blood-crazed Greeks without a thought of fear, and looked on the most horrible sights with a steady eye. But now I had my family with me. Nervous of every shadow, and startled at every distant sound, I stole carefully through back-alleys and deserted side-streets.

Suddenly there were running footsteps behind us. My father clutched at me and urgently hissed, 'Run, Aeneas, run! They've nearly got us!' For the first time that day, I panicked. I rushed blindly up streets and down, blood pounding behind my eyes. I could vaguely feel Iulus' fingers digging into my palm, and hear him plaintively crying that he could not keep up with me.

Somehow we reached the temple of Ceres. My faithful servants were there, and numbers of our friends. I set my father down, eased the stiffness from my shoulders, passed Iulus to his nurse, and looked round to smile at my wife. She was not there.

I remembered that moment of panic. Did I lose her then? I raced back to the spot, yelling her name, not caring who heard me. No sign of her. Like a beast in a maze I charged in and out of the streets. The fighting was mostly over. Piles of valuables looted from Trojan homes were heaped up here and there. The glow from a hundred dying fires revealed long lines of terrified women and bewildered children, rounded up for the slave-market. I only noticed that Creusa was not among them. I thought

of home. Perhaps she had found her way there? No use, the Greeks had broken in; the house was a silent ruin.

I don't know how long I would have gone on searching. I was about to drop in despair, when I heard her voice. She seemed to be standing before me, larger than life, but otherwise her usual calm, sweet self. 'Don't worry about me, darling. I am safe. The Greeks will never find me now. You must go on. The gods mean you to sail to a western land, the rich land by the River Tiber. This is to be your people's home. There you must marry a Latin princess, and found a race that will rule the earth. Stop thinking of Creusa now . . .'

I tried to hold her. I wanted to clasp her, to tell her that I did not want any foreign princess, that no new land could be mine without her. But her ghost slipped through my outstretched arms and was gone.

I went back to my friends, greeted a large number of new arrivals, comforted Iulus, and carried my father to a safe hiding-place in the hills."

III The Wanderings of the Trojans

AENEAS paused in his story. The banquet guests were silent. Dido sat quite still.

"All winter our people worked at ship-building, and by spring we were ready to sail. Twenty good ships were built, and loaded with supplies of food and wine, and small bundles of private belongings salvaged from the sack of Troy. It was hard work, organizing everything — but at least it kept us too busy to ask questions about our destination.

So we sailed, and before long reached Thrace, a land not far from Troy, where King Priam had ties of friendship. There were no unlucky signs, and so we surveyed a plot of ground for our settlement. I began to feel happy, and, in response to the wishes of my grateful people, agreed to call our new home 'Aenea'.

Everyone gathered round to watch me sink my spade into the earth, and pronounce the city's name. I chose a spot where the roots of a young tree broke the hard surface of the ground. Driving in the spade, I grasped the sapling and tore it out.

Some say that trees have guardian spirits. I know only this, that the scream that came from the wounded soil was

34

human. We clutched one another in horror, and stared at the hole. Dark blood bubbled up from its centre, and oozed towards my feet. 'Stop, Aeneas!' The words spurted from the soil. 'This is a wicked land – no home for Trojans! You must know me – I am Polydorus!'

We all gasped at hearing the name. Polydorus had been sent by King Priam to seek help from the Thracian king during the war, but had not returned in time. Lucky man, we had thought.

'Aeneas, Aeneas, a cruel tyrant rules this land. I came protected by the laws of hospitality, but he killed me, and left my corpse to rot dishonoured here on the shore. If you stay here, you will all be murdered. Leave this land; spare only a moment to calm my tortured spirit.'

People were already running towards the sea. The ships were afloat, and the anchors weighed, almost before I had completed the sacred rites and laid the ghost of Polydorus to rest.

Our course now lay southwards, to Apollo's holy island, Delos. My father was keen to make this our next landing, for his friend King Anius would make us welcome in Delos, and there we could consult Apollo's oracle.

Delos was a charming island. Anius greeted my father most warmly, and entertained us all with every comfort. As soon as I could slip away, I hurried to the temple of Apollo. 'Show us a place of refuge, O Lord,' I prayed, 'Grant a haven to the weary survivors of your faithful Trojan people. O Apollo, you who can see beyond the sight of men, tell us where our new home must be.'

As I finished speaking, the floor under my feet began to sway. The stone blocks of the temple walls rattled like pebbles shaken by a giant hand. I could not tell whether the voice I heard was around me or within me; but I expect you all know how it is when a god gives his answer.

'Seek out your first mother, Aeneas. Your first mother!' These words the oracle spoke.

What would you make of that? I was no stranger to the dark sayings of oracles, but this meant nothing to me. I consulted with my father: 'Perhaps it is the Earth? The Earth is often called the first mother of the human race. But how could we *seek out* the Earth, when we walk on it all our lives?'

My father, however, had a different idea. 'I think the god wants us to trace back to the beginnings of our race. We must make for the *first mother* of the Trojan people.'

'Troy is gone, sir,' I said impatiently. I hoped my old father was not seizing an excuse to return to the past.

'Be quiet, boy. I still have my wits. Now think − who is the ancestor of our people?'

'Teucer,' I answered automatically.

'Good. And Teucer was not born in Troy, was he? He sailed to Asia from . . . ?'

'From Crete. Crete? Is Crete our promised homeland?' Somehow I had never thought of Crete, with its tales of bull-worship and labyrinths and human sacrifice.

'It must be Crete, Aeneas. Remember, in Crete they pray to the Earth-goddess, the Great Mother.'

So we sailed at once for Crete. In the three days that the journey took I almost convinced myself that this was the right place for us. We disembarked. I selected a site. We marked out the boundaries. I formally named our new city 'Pergamea', after the old citadel of Troy. Work began. I called a council to frame policy and laws.

I was not really surprised when the first disturbing

reports came in. The newly-planted crops were wilting; the soil was drying up and cracking; the cattle were refusing to eat. When the people began to sicken, I drew my father aside for a private talk.

'Perhaps the oracle was wrong, sir.'

'Never, Aeneas. Apollo cannot lie. It is sinful to think such a thing.'

'But we are only human. We may not have interpreted the holy words correctly. Perhaps *your first mother* didn't mean Crete at all?'

'Well, then, Aeneas, the only thing to do is to return to Delos and ask the oracle again,' my father said finally.

I certainly did not welcome the prospect of retracing our steps. I was eager to arrive, not to wander for years on end. I went to bed that night still turning the problem over in my mind. I thought of one island after another, trying to make one of them fit the terms of the oracle. I must have dropped off at last into a fitful sleep.

My quarters consisted of a makeshift hut, one of the first buildings of our ill-fated settlement. Opposite my bed I had set up the images of our home-gods. Now, as I tossed and wrestled with the riddle in my mind, it seemed to my feverish brain that the statues' eyes began to glow, and that their lips moved and spoke.

'Listen to us, Aeneas. We are your home-gods, whom you rescued from the flames of Troy. We have not forgotten your devotion. You deserve our help. We know the true meaning of Apollo's words.'

'Then tell me!'

'Your *first mother*, Aeneas, is the land of your ancestor, Dardanus. He came from a western land called Italy. Italy is your promised home, Aeneas. Crete is forbidden to you.'

Should he stop listening to his Dad?

I awoke with the word 'Italy' humming in my ears. I went straight to my father.

'What you say is true, Aeneas,' he admitted, after a short silence. 'Our ancestor, Dardanus, did come from Italy. My mind was on a different branch of the family. Teucer came from a separate line.' He paused in thought again, and then added, 'You know, that poor girl Cassandra used to say we would end up in Italy, but who ever listened to her?'

We had no difficulty in persuading our people to abandon settlement on Crete. They accepted the news about Italy with willing hearts, and once more we put out to sea.

Almost at once we struck bad weather. We were buffeted by gales; thick storm-clouds hid the horizon by day, and the stars by night. My steersman, Palinurus, had to confess himself at a loss. We hove to and rode out the storm until the skies cleared.

On the fourth day we sighted land. Closer inspection revealed a nest of islands known as the Strophades, not far from Greece. At least we had been blown in the right direction. The place seemed pleasant enough for a short stop; there were some cattle wandering about to supply us with a meal.

Not till dinner was actually sizzling on our plates did the monsters appear. First we heard them − a whirring, whining noise like the onslaught of a thousand giant mosquitoes. And then we felt their savage claws, their furiously beating wings, and their foul, disgusting droppings.

You may have heard tales of the Harpies, ghastly creatures, half woman, half bird of prey, who force poor

wretches to starve to death in a land of plenty. There was no question of our eating any of the food now; what they had not seized was buried under a vile, stinking mess. We snatched up weapons and lunged at them again and again. They only shrieked more piercingly, flapped their wings and made off into the sky. All but their leader, Celaeno, who perched on a high rock and screeched down at us: 'Do you dare to come to the Harpies' land, and steal our food? The gods sent you to Italy — to Italy you will go, but then beware! Famine will punish you there; you will be forced to chew at your own tables. You will remember the Harpies then!' She flew away. Crying on the gods to avert this evil omen, we ran to the ships.

Our course now took us up the coast of Greece, a land we had reason to hate. We stared hard as we passed Ithaca, the island of false Ulysses, and wondered whether he was safe at home, enjoying the plunder and glory he had won at Troy. Since winter was near, we put in at Actium, on the north coast, and camped till the weather would let us sail again.

The seasons, at least, can be trusted, and in the spring we reached the coastal town of Buthrotum. I wanted to check the truth of an extraordinary rumour: that this Greek city was ruled by the Trojan Helenus, son of Priam, who had somehow married his sister-in-law, Hector's widow, Andromache.

No sooner had we landed than I saw her, Andromache, once the beloved wife of our greatest warrior. Day after day she had climbed the battlements of Troy, her baby in her arms, to watch Hector go out to defy the Greeks. She had stood quiet among the wailing women, the day they brought Hector's body home.

She recognized me at once. Rising from her knees (for she had been making a tomb-offering), she took me by both wrists, and looked me over slowly. 'It is you, Aeneas, son of Anchises. I am glad to see you alive.' There was little gladness in her words. The only man who really mattered was dead; living men were all much the same.

'The gods have preserved us both, Andromache,' I replied, in tones as formal as hers. 'Permit me to ask, are you still the − servant − of Pyrrhus?'

At the sound of that name, her lips tightened. She jerked herself away from me and spoke, her voice low and even, her eyes fixed on the sea: 'Even Pyrrhus was mortal. After he had killed my father and my brothers in Troy, he selected me to be his happy bride. I bore him two children. When he grew tired of me, he passed me on to his slave. I was lucky. The slave was Hector's brother, Helenus. He had not been killed, because he was a priest. Pyrrhus was eventually stabbed by Agamemnon's mad son, Orestes. Sometimes the gods are just.'

'Is Helenus still here, then?'

'He is king. Part of the kingdom came to him after Pyrrhus died. We live quietly. Helenus is planning to make the country a model of old Troy.'

We walked a little in silence, sharing memories too painful to speak of. Several times she looked at me as if to ask something.

'What is it, Andromache?' She stood still, and turned to me. There were tears on her face now.

'Is your little boy . . . ? Is Ascanius with you?'

'Yes.' I remembered hearing that Ulysses had flung Andromache's baby boy, Astyanax, from Troy's highest tower, shouting that no son of Hector would ever grow up to avenge his father.

'I'm glad,' she said.

It was a relief to see Helenus coming to meet us. He welcomed me heartily, led me to the city, and showed off the towers and streets and temples, all built in exact imitation of Troy. I kissed the gate respectfully, but my heart was now longing for a land across the sea.

We stayed a few days, out of courtesy. Then, hoping the moment was right, I approached our host. 'Helenus,' I said, 'we are deeply grateful to you for your kindness to us. Allow me to ask one more favour, and then we must set sail. You are Apollo's priest; please use your prophetic powers, and tell me what dangers we must still face. I believe that the gods want us to settle in Italy, but there may yet be fearful horrors lying in wait for us. I must know all I can.'

Helenus was pleased to help. His dark, intense eyes reminded me of Cassandra, but he had none of her troubled restlessness. The holy sacrifice seemed to make him especially calm: he spoke Apollo's secret knowledge in a firm and steady voice: 'Your voyage to Italy will take place as foretold, Aeneas, but do not think that the journey is short. You must not settle on the east coast, nearest here, for it is filled with your enemies, the Greeks. Sail around Italy until you reach the land Jupiter has ordained to be yours. You must steer through the waters of Sicily, but avoid the narrow strait. There ships are swallowed by the monster Scylla or, if they try to escape her, gulped down by the swirling torrent of Charybdis. Be sure of one thing: do not forget to worship Juno. Win her favour, if you can.'

I pressed Helenus for one further point. 'How will we know when we have arrived?'

For a moment his face grew rigid. I was afraid that he might refuse to say any more. 'There are things, Aeneas, that the gods forbid me to reveal, but this, you may know. When you reach Italy, go to Cumae. Look for a priestess called the Sibyl. Consult her; she knows vital truths about your people. Some day after that, you will come to a river, and near its bank you will find a large, white sow with thirty piglets. There will be the site for your city.'

So – such majestic prophecies, such a grand and noble quest would end in a litter of pigs! Sometimes it is hard to trust the gods.

We prepared the ships. Helenus saw us off, presenting us with generous gifts. Andromache insisted on giving Iulus a beautiful cloak she had made herself. Her own little boy would have been exactly his age.

We sailed now by the shortest route, Palinurus steering with a sure eye and a steady hand. The second dawn at sea brought our first sight of Italy. We gathered on the decks to gaze at the distant coastline, all with our private dreams. My father spoke for us all. Lifting high a bowl of wine as a thank-offering to the gods, he prayed for fair winds and a calm passage.

Soon we were close enough to pick out rocks, trees, houses and temples. This was no uninhabited land. I saw four white horses, grazing peacefully in a field. When I pointed them out to my father, however, he exclaimed: 'War, Aeneas! Such horses are bred for war. This is a land of battles. But in time, perhaps, even war-horses can be trained to pull a plough.'

I had constantly in mind Helenus' warning about Juno,

so I insisted on a sacrifice there and then, as we sailed alongside the shore. As we rounded the southern point of the coast and aimed the ships towards Sicily, we could hear a curious noise, loud roaring and violent sucking. I remembered Scylla, the dog-faced monster-maiden, and Charybdis, the fatal whirlpool.

'Pull at the oars!' I cried to the men. 'Row for your lives!'

We forced the ships south, and put in, exhausted, on the shore near Mount Etna, whose peak towers over the coast of Sicily. This place made us uneasy, with its strange rumbling and shaking, and the bursts of smoke that bruised and stained the sky. We spent the night huddled in the woods, looking forward to dawn and sailing away.

The morning brought a surprise. A ragged, filthy figure of a man emerged from the bushes and begged us to let him sail with us. He was unmistakably a Greek soldier, rather less sure of himself than others we had met. 'I know you are Trojans,' he gasped, flinging his thin, tattered body at our feet. 'Kill me if you like — but don't leave me here.' My good old father held out his hand at once, and told him not to be afraid. I hung back a little, remembering Sinon.

'I was sailing home from Troy with my king, the famous Ulysses. Things didn't go too well, and we put in here for some rest and supplies. Some of us went exploring to see who lived in the caves up there. Well, we found out all right. An enormous ogre, a Cyclops, with one huge eye in the middle of his forehead. He trapped us in his cave and set about eating us, two at a time, morning and evening. You have to believe me — he crushed full-grown warriors between his teeth like nutshells, and swallowed them, hair, bones, and all. That's the way we'd all have gone, but for

Ulysses' cunning. He got the monster drunk and, while he lay there, belching out wine and human guts, we put out his eye with a sharpened stake. Next morning, when he let out the sheep he kept in the cave, he wasn't to know that we were hanging on to their fleece underneath. No one ever had brains like Ulysses, that's for sure. They all got away in the ships — all but me. I was left behind. I've spent three months hiding in the woods, nearly starved, eating only roots and berries, keeping out of their way. You see, the creature who caught us isn't the only one. There are at least a hundred Cyclops-monsters living here. Quick, sir, you must get away right now! Yours is the first human face I've seen in three months of terror: if you kill me for being a Greek, I don't care! At least I'll die at human hands, no worse than the risk I took at Troy.'

We could feel the earth rumbling. The sky was growing dark. Our eyes flew to the smoking peak of Mount Etna, but this was no volcanic eruption. Lumbering down the slope, each unsteady footstep rocking the earth, the blind Cyclops was groping towards the shore. His huge head blotted out the sun. We stood frozen as he shambled past us, waded into the sea and bathed the yawning hole in his forehead. Red streaks appeared in the waves.

We moved. Silently we slipped to the ships, hauling the wretched Greek on board with us, cut the cables, and heaved at the oars. The Cyclops heard, and plunged towards us through water several fathoms deep, bellowing with rage. But we had a head start, and were soon out of reach.

Round the southern coast of Sicily we steered, so as to avoid the strait of Scylla and Charybdis, and put in at Drepanum at the western end. And it was there, with just a short way left to go, that my father, noble Anchises, passed away. No seer, no oracle, no vision had foretold this agony, the greatest I could suffer.

A day out at sea, and we were hit by the storm that drove us here to Carthage. The rest of my story you know, gracious Queen."

Aeneas had finished. For some time Dido and her guests sat silent.

IV The Tragedy of Queen Dido

QUEEN Dido had no idea that in her heart she bore
a dangerous, festering wound, the sly work of Cupid's invisible arrow. She knew only that she shook with fever all
night, and dreamt confused and frightening dreams.

The next morning she spoke to her sister, Anna. As
Queen, Dido had few people she could trust. Now she sat
on her bed, her face strangely flushed and her palms
pressed to her knees. Her words tumbled out unsteadily.

"I had fearful dreams last night, Anna. Do you believe
they mean disaster? Did you notice our guest at dinner?
He has the broadest shoulders — you can tell he's the son
of a goddess. I keep thinking about his terrible suffering.
Anna, do you know, if I hadn't sworn to love Sychaeus
forever, if I could ever be free to marry again — what
am I saying? Anna, don't listen to me, I must be going
mad. I swore a public oath before Sychaeus' tomb.
Everyone heard me, including the almighty gods. I am still
married to Sychaeus, as much now as on our wedding day.
If I ever betrayed him, I should deserve to die!" Dido's
final words were lost in an outburst of sobbing.

Anna reached out to her sister in sympathy, and waited
for the tears to subside. She chose her words carefully;
Anna was not clever, but a lifetime as Dido's sister had

taught her a kind of wisdom. "Dido," she said, "we all know how you value honour. Of course you could spend the rest of your life married to a tomb, but aren't you being selfish? You have refused the love of all the African chieftains, even Iarbas, the grandest of them all. You've proved your loyalty to Sychaeus. Now you should think of your people."

"What do you mean?" The Queen was looking up now.

"Here we are, in a strange land, surrounded by hostile tribes. You've done wonders, Dido, but what if there's a war? What if our brother Pygmalion comes after us? Isn't it time Carthage had a strong man to lead her army? Have you thought what a mighty nation we could become if the Trojans joined us and settled here?"

Anna paused long enough to look at Dido's flushed face and trembling, clutching fingers. Confidently now, she went on: "Pray to the gods to release you from your vow. They are not cruel, and Juno has always favoured you. You have served her long enough to prove your devotion. This stormy weather is just what we need; the Trojans won't be sailing till the spring."

Dido had heard enough. Within the hour the Queen's orders were ringing through the palace — a special day of offerings and prayers to the heavenly gods, with particular devotion to Juno. The courtiers remarked on the Queen's excellent sense of piety, and bustled about with preparations, selecting perfect beasts for sacrifice and decking the altars with flowers.

It seemed to Dido that the ceremonies calmed her spirit. She arranged a tour of the city for her guests, and chattered gaily and long to Aeneas about the splendid plans for great temples, public squares, impenetrable walls and lofty towers. She hardly heard her own words, knowing only what her heart was speaking.

With friendly good-byes they returned to their own quarters. But Dido found herself inventing empty messages to be delivered to Aeneas urgently, and then cancelled them in shame. She showered gifts on the delighted Iulus, and then locked herself away to cry on her bed. The business of Carthage was forgotten; impatient officials were told that the Queen was unable to see them; the people wondered at her absence from state ceremonies. Left without instructions, workmen abandoned the building-sites: the shadows of half-finished towers grew long across the city.

High in the home of the gods, Juno was well aware of the change in her favourite city. She approached Venus directly. "Well done!" Juno began, "You have managed to overwhelm a poor mortal with your divine power! What now? Why don't we make a bargain, you and I? Let us arrange a marriage: then Dido can enjoy that love you know so much about, and my Carthage can flourish with a strong king by the Queen's side."

Venus smiled: "I'm sure you know best. As Jupiter's mighty queen, you must know what the Fates intend. If it is decreed that Trojans and Carthaginians must rule a joint kingdom, then go ahead."

Juno replied quickly: "You can leave all that to me. My proposal is this: tomorrow Dido and Aeneas are planning a hunting-party in the woods. While they are out, I shall arrange a sudden cloudburst. Everyone will scatter for cover and our happy couple will make for the same cave. A perfect setting for a wedding. As goddess of marriage, I shall see that everything is done properly — if you have no objection."

Venus bit back another smile, and nodded.

Day came, and a laughing, gaily-dressed crowd gathered for the hunt. Barking hounds frisked about, slaves clattered to and fro with spears and nets, and young men showed off their keen horses, proud and anxious to prove their courage. Iulus, astride his first real mount, galloped back and forth, rehearsing fearsome war-cries for the lion and wild boar he hoped to meet. Dido's horse stood pawing the ground, a magnificent beast with harness of purple and gold. The Queen's outfit was also purple and gold, down to the buckle in her hair and the quiver of arrows slung over her shoulder. As for Aeneas, his rich garments suited his graceful, godlike figure.

The rumbling began when they were quite some way from the city. Gay laughter turned to cries of alarm as the sky darkened, and hailstones struck fiercely and rapidly at unprotected heads and bodies. "Run!" came the general call, and people made for bushes, huts, overhanging rocks, any shelter they could reach. The Queen of Carthage and the Trojan leader took refuge in a nearby cave.

Then Mother Earth herself gave a signal; Juno appeared as matron-of-honour. In the sky lightning flared like wedding-torches, and a choir of mountain-nymphs wailed an eerie hymn. Aeneas looked out and saw only a storm, but Dido's distorted mind formed everything into a ceremony of marriage. No need now, she thought, to fret about her reputation. Her vow was forgotten. It was marriage she lived in now, not sin.

Almost at once, Rumour began to fly about. Rumour is a dreadful monster, full of feathers, and eyes, and tongues and ears. It screams through the world at night, and watches from roof-tops by day, never silent, always

squawking a mixture of truth and lies. This Rumour spread swiftly through the tribes of North Africa, crying: "A Trojan wanderer, Aeneas, has come visiting Carthage. Dido has given up everything for him. They're spending all winter wallowing in disgusting orgies, never giving a thought to their royal duties. What a shocking scandal!"

Among the African chieftains who heard the spiteful words of Rumour was Iarbas, richest and most powerful of them all, and, some said, a son of Jupiter himself. Iarbas, whose own proposals to Dido had received hardly a polite reply, cursed in jealous rage, and cried out to the mighty King of heaven, "Is this all I get for my life-long devotion to the gods? Is that Trojan pansy going to make a fool of me? If so, I'll call Jupiter's power nothing but empty rumour!"

His words were heard. Almighty Jupiter turned his gaze to the walls of Carthage, and at once beckoned Mercury, the quicksilver messenger of the gods: "Fly down to Carthage, my son, and deliver these words to the Trojan leader. This is not the future he was born to have; this is not why he survived the ruin of Troy. His race is destined to rule Italy, a nation bursting with power and exulting in war, and to conquer the world and unite it under one law. If such a glorious destiny is nothing to him, does he mean to deprive his son of its splendour? Why is he wasting his time with a nation which is to be no friend of his? That is all; give him this message from me."

Mercury slipped on his winged sandals, and picked up the staff that was his token as herald of the gods. It assured him safe passage anywhere, even to the dreaded kingdom of the dead. His journey to Carthage took only a moment.

Aeneas, richly cloaked and wearing a bejewelled sword

that was Dido's gift, was discussing plans for the building of Carthage. Round him Trojan and Carthaginian officers were absorbed in argument. Only Aeneas noticed the shimmering figure. His ears alone heard the taunting words: "Well, then, here we are, busy building a city for our lady-friend! What about your own work? The father of gods and men has noticed a little – shall we say – slackness? I have been sent to tell you this: even if you have forgotten all about your own glorious future, how about giving some thought to your son's? You owe him an Italian kingdom and a place called Rome."

The silvery form of Mercury never stood quite still, and before Aeneas could fully grasp its presence, it was gone. The Carthaginians, deep in discussion, did not notice Aeneas' pale, horrified stare. They barely heard his muttered apology and abrupt departure.

Aeneas struggled to master himself. His first impulse was to rush to Dido, and pour out to her all his shock and guilt. But what would Dido say? How could he explain to her that he must leave at once? She would never believe that he had heard a command from heaven. How could he expect her to accept such a story?

He summoned his trusted captains. "Men, there's been a change of plan," he said briskly, "We're sailing at once. Get your ships ready, and rouse the crew. But do it quietly – no alarm. The less the locals know, the faster we can sail." He hoped for some protest, some word of regret from one of them, some request for more time. But they were clearly delighted, and hurried away to obey.

All he had to do now was to tell Dido. He practised phrase after phrase in his mind, and made his way slowly to the palace.

In the end, however, he had no need to say anything. Rumour, swiftest of all creatures, had reached the palace well before him. The Queen was waiting.

"Did you think you could just slip away?" she screamed as he entered. The shrill voice belonged to a woman betrayed, not to the Queen of Carthage. "Never mind your wife! Never mind your marriage vows! Are you so desperate to leave that you'll set sail in this winter weather? And for an unknown land! Would you even sail back to Troy in this season? Is it something I have done? See, I'm begging you now — for the sake of everything we've been to each other, if I've ever helped you in the slightest way, change your mind. Think what fate you're leaving me to suffer: because of you, all the tribes of Africa hate me, and even my own people resent me now. I gave up for you the dearest thing I had — my vow to Sychaeus. My reputation is gone. You're leaving me to my murderous brother. Or would you prefer me to beg for the mercy of some savage chief? What can I call you — deserter? husband? guest? If only, if only we could have had a son, a little Aeneas who could remind me of you . . ." Dido's words faded into the silence of despair.

Aeneas had to speak. His voice showed little emotion. "Your majesty, I would never deny nor forget what you have done for me and my people. As long as I live, I shall speak your name with honour. But let me, madam, make a few points about this matter: you are mistaken. I have not been planning a secret escape. I am not your husband; we have never been married. If the Fates had been kind to me, I should still be living in Troy with my family. But instead, I am summoned to Italy. Apollo's oracles, visions and dreams every night, the ghost of my father Anchises, and now a heavenly messenger — all of them cry the same word: 'Italy'. You, of all people, should understand what drives a man to seek his own land. Please stop tormenting me. Italy is my destiny, not my choice!"

Aeneas bowed formally as he finished. Avoiding the Queen's unbelieving stare, he turned to go.

"Stop!" It was a Queen's anger that commanded him now. "I have something to say to you before you go. You have shown not a moment of human compassion, so how can I believe your claims to divine or noble parentage? No, you were born of stone, nursed by the heartless cliffs and brought up by wild beasts. I have been too trusting. I saved you and your crew from death and raised you to a high place in my kingdom. And, in return, what is my reward? The gods command you to depart? Well, I will not detain you. Off you go, chase your Italian kingdom. I only hope that one day you will regret this, that when it is too late, you will call out my name. You can be sure that I will come. My spirit will be there to taunt you as you die in agony. Your punishment is waiting."

Dido did not stay for any reply. Her departure was regal. She swept through the doorway, stopped, and suddenly fainted. Her horrified ladies carried her to the bedroom.

Aeneas stood alone for a few moments, desperate to offer her comfort, his heart melting with love. Then, sighing deeply, he left the palace. He went down to the harbour and sharply ordered the men to be speedier. The slightest delay was impossible.

Anna came from the palace with a message for him: the Queen was asking the Trojan leader to re-consider the hazards of winter sailing; a short delay would ensure a safe journey. The Queen reminded the noble Trojan prince that she was guilty of no crimes against his people, and that he had no cause to vent his anger against her. The Queen promised the royal hero that she would never again mention marriage; she only requested a few days to calm her troubled spirit.

Aeneas heard all these requests without expression or comment. "Thank the Queen for her concern, but our arrangements cannot be altered now," he said eventually.

Dido now spent all her time before the altars of the gods, performing the sacred rites, and examining the offerings. When she saw the wine turn to blood, she was not even surprised. She hung decorations on the memorial to Sychaeus, and listened for long hours to the voice she could hear calling from the tomb. Finally she spoke, no longer frantic, to her sister:

"Anna, I remember once meeting a witch who told me how to destroy the spell of an evil love. She taught me the ritual — what words to say and what herbs to mix. You must help me: it is very important to prepare a bonfire in secret and burn up everything that could remind me of that man: his clothes, his armour, and especially our bed. Once they are all gone, I shall be free of him forever."

Anna, in great relief, hurried away to make preparations. Dido approached the altars once more and called on the gods — but now she was not praying to the heavenly powers. She invoked Darkness and Chaos, Hecate the witch-queen, and the pale Moon-maiden. She mixed herbs plucked by moonlight with poisonous syrup, and prayed for death.

The night was peaceful. All the country slept, all creatures of the fields, of air and water. Dido alone struggled with her final questions, "Should I become the bride of a nomad chief? Should I sail after the Trojan fleet? Better die; it's what I deserve for betraying Sychaeus."

On the Trojan flagship, Aeneas slept, all preparations made for an early departure, but his dreams were invaded roughly by the shining figure of Mercury. "How can you sleep? Can't you hear the friendly breezes? Get moving! She's plotting some new form of torture for you. You can't trust a woman."

Aeneas started. He was fully awake, but there was no one with him; Mercury had vanished. He roused his officers and crew. "Man the oars! We're sailing!" There was a general cheer. Each sailor took his appointed place. Aeneas cut the mooring-rope with a single blow of his sword. The ships began to slip out of the harbour. No lanterns shone. Aeneas stood on the prow, his arm around his son, and prayed with all his heart, "Lead on, you heavenly powers. Protect us from harm and grant us safe passage."

The first rays of dawn revealed the empty harbour, and the open sea dotted with sails. No one needed to tell Dido the news; she saw it for herself from the palace window. Was this man going to make a fool of her? She rushed to the door, ready to order the fastest ships of Carthage to give chase. But she did not speak the words of command; instead, she sank to the floor, a hopeless and bitter figure of a Queen, and addressed her own reflexion in the marble paving which glinted at her in cold mockery:

"It's too late, Dido. You should have thought more clearly before you handed him your kingdom. Too bad that you believed his stories of faith and devotion. You could have had him torn to pieces when he landed.

You could have slaughtered his son and carved up his corpse for the table. That would have been more fitting."

She rose unsteadily and crossed to the window. The spreading sails could still be seen, but they were smaller now. Dido raised her eyes to the sky: "Mighty Sun, Juno my guardian, goddesses of the night and avenging Furies, hear my final prayers. If Fate has decreed that he must reach land safely, then let him never enjoy it in peace. Let him be torn by wars and the loss of his dearest friends, and send him an early, dishonourable death. This is my last prayer — I offer it with my blood."

Dido's gaze turned now to the rooftops of the city she had loved: "People of Carthage, hate his race forever! Bring forth a hero to avenge my wrongs, to beat them low, and destroy them with fire and sword. Fight them, my people, father and son, enemies to the end of time!"

Dido called an old servant, and sent her to tell Anna that it was time to begin the solemn ritual of purification. The woman bustled away importantly, and Dido flung open the doors of the inner courtyard.

Anna had, as usual, carried out her instructions faithfully. A large wood-heap had been prepared, and piled on top were some clothes Aeneas had left, his armour, and the royal bed.

Dido paused no longer. She pulled herself up onto the pyre, and grasped Aeneas' sword. "I have accomplished a little. My city walls stand firm, my husband's death is avenged. I could have been happy, but the Fates were against me."

Her ladies, wearing holy garlands on their heads, stood ready with torches flaming. Dido motioned them to set the pyre alight, and they, cowed by the look in the Queen's eyes, obeyed. Dido raised the sword, "Look hard at this smoke, Aeneas," she cried, "and bear forever the curse of my death!"

The shriek of women echoed from the walls. At once Rumour careered about the palace, till all was spinning in commotion. Anna burst into the couryard. Ignoring the flames, she plucked her sister from the pyre and pressed her robes against the flowing wound. She repeated Dido's name, staunching the blood, hugging her to her own breast, calling for water, cursing her own stupidity.

Dido made a last effort to speak, but could only gasp. Her eyes were rolling wildly, taking in the sky, the walls, the pyre, her sister's face.

It was great Juno who took pity on Dido's final agony, and sent her servant Iris to bring Dido relief. Iris flew down in a sweeping arc, leaving a trail of rainbow hues in her wake, and whispered soothing words to the dying Queen. Then she cut a lock of Dido's hair, and set her spirit free.

V The Trojans Stop in Sicily

AENEAS' ships sped before the wind. Looking back at the distant towers of Carthage, he saw a faint smear of black smoke rising to the sky. His companions followed his gaze, but only young Iulus exclaimed and pointed at the brilliant rainbow now stretched over the coastline, making the column of smoke stand out thin and stark. The adults exchanged silent glances, and Aeneas fixed his eyes on the open sea ahead, willing Italy to appear quickly.

"Message from the steersman, sir. Will you go up and speak with him at once, if you can, sir?"

Glad to be distracted, Aeneas hurried to the stern and found Palinurus studying a mass of clouds that hovered some distance before them. They were very dark, and the sea beneath them looked shadowed and unwelcoming.

"Storm ahead, sir," the steersman explained. "Looks like a bad squall. Could hit us badly if we sail straight through it."

"Try. We must make all speed to Italy." Aeneas succeeded in sounding firm. Palinurus frowned, but did not argue. The air grew chill; the sea was grey now all around. The sails began an urgent flapping. Something tore.

"Gale's too strong for sailing, sir."

"Then row!" retorted Aeneas. To quell his own fear, he

flung himself onto a bench and grabbed the end of an oar. For an hour the crew strained and sweated at oars that lurched out of their hands, while the ship spun helplessly in a whirling sea.

"We can make Sicily, sir," urged Palinurus. "The nearby coast is friendly, and we don't want to chance another shipwreck."

"No, we do not. Very well, steersman, bear east. It seems the gods will not be kind to us." Then, seeing the man's downcast face, Aeneas added, "It's not your fault, Palinurus. You did your best. You never know, this landing could be a blessing. As you said, this coast of Sicily is friendly, and personally very dear to me, since it holds my father's grave."

Soon they were beaching the ships on the peaceful sand, and exchanging greetings with old Acestes, ruler of the local settlement, whose mother had been of Trojan blood. Acestes welcomed them with hearty hospitality, and provided food and shelter at once for the weary travellers.

Early the next morning, Aeneas summoned all the Trojans to a meeting on the beach. He watched them gather, walking slowly in small groups, trusting but down-hearted. "How much longer can they keep their faith in me?" he wondered. "I have given them nothing but setbacks."

When the stretch of sand was quite crowded, Aeneas climbed a nearby hillock and raised his arms. "Friends," he called, "this is a very fortunate landing. It is exactly twelve months since royal Anchises, my honoured father, was laid to rest here on this coast. The gods have sent us here today to honour his memory with celebrations. Our good kinsman Acestes has generously donated two splendid oxen for every ship. We shall devote eight days to sacrifice and dedication, and on the ninth day hold a festival of sports and games. There will be something for everyone — rowing, running, archery and boxing! I shall provide the prizes!"

A buzz of cheerful excitement broke out among the crowd. Youths were exchanging good-natured punches, and some of the older men were flexing their muscles to the friendly teasing of their comrades. Aeneas felt some of his secret worries lifting from his heart. After a few moments he called again for silence. "Let us put on holy garlands."

Aeneas put a myrtle wreath on his own head, and was followed by his son and their host, Acestes. All the others did the same. In a long and silent procession, the Trojans moved to the site of Anchises' grave. There Aeneas poured on to the soil two goblets of wine, two of milk, and two of ox-blood. Then he scattered blossoms about the grave, and addressed in reverent words the spirit of his beloved father.

Hardly had he begun to pray, "Greetings, O sacred ashes of my father, prevented by fate from reaching the shores of Italy . . ." when a huge snake slid out from the tomb and glided to taste the ritual foods. The people watched breathlessly, but it only drank its fill, and returned peacefully to its lair under the tomb. Aeneas, suspecting that the snake was his father's guardian spirit, continued the ceremony with redoubled zeal. He slaughtered two sheep, two pigs and two young bulls, and invoked once more the spirit of the dead. The offerings made, the Trojans began to roast the carcasses over their cooking-fires. The air filled with the scent of roasting meat.

The ninth day dawned at last. Spectators for the games streamed in from nearby towns and villages, attracted by the fine weather and rumours of excitement. The Trojan ladies withdrew, as was their custom, leaving the games to the men.

A trumpet-blast signalled the opening event, a rowing-race, to be contested by four fast Trojan ships, each manned by a crew of champion oarsmen. As the captains drew lots for positions, the herald announced the names of the competing ships: "*Whale*, captained by Mnestheus, *Chimaera*, captained by Gyas, *Centaur*, captained by Sergestus, and *Scylla*, captained by Cloanthus. Competitors will row as far as the rock directly opposite, marked clearly by the leafy tree-trunk, turn, and row to the starting-line. Rowers, take your oars!"

The crowd was hushed. The captains stood prominently on the afterdecks, the steersmen placed expert hands on the tillers, the crews, their muscles taut and glistening with oil, crouched over the oars. The trumpet blew a long, clear blast.

In an instant the calm sea became a churning cauldron of white foam and spray, almost hiding the boats from the lines of yelling spectators. The huge *Chimaera* took the lead, followed closely by the *Scylla*. Some distance behind, the *Whale* and the *Centaur* were vying fiercely to avoid the last place.

Almost at the rock, the *Chimaera* was still leading, when her captain, Gyas, shouted anxiously to his steersman, "Closer to the rock! Bring her in closer!" But the steersman, fearing a hidden reef, kept well in deep water. At that moment *Scylla*'s steersman seized his chance, and slipping in between *Chimaera* and the rock, made a triumphant turn. Her captain, Cloanthus, laughed merrily at Gyas' furious expression, and waved cheekily as they

passed. Gyas, boiling with frustration, grabbed his unfortunate steersman, heaved him overboard, and seized the
tiller himself. The crews of the *Whale* and the *Centaur*,
toiling at their oars, found time to chuckle at *Chimaera*'s
steersman clambering on to the rock, blowing and spitting
out salt-water and bad language.

Mnestheus, captain of the *Whale*, strode restlessly
among the benches, urging his perspiring crew to try
harder. "Never mind victory! Just don't come last!" Luck
was on their side, for the *Centaur*, edging in to get closest
to the rock, suddenly met a jutting reef. There was a
splintering crash, and *Centaur* was out of the race.
Encouraged by this stroke of fortune, *Whale*'s crew in-
creased their efforts. They were now in clear water, with a
fresh wind at their back, and were gaining on the enormous
Chimaera which was now feeling the loss of her proper
steersman. Gyas was doing his best, but his lack of experi-
ence was showing.

Now only *Scylla*, captained by Cloanthus, lay ahead of
the *Whale*. The spectators were in a riot of noisy excitement. Cloanthus, seeing defeat only seconds away, cried a
desperate prayer to the sea-gods. Instantly his ship felt the
blast of a mighty, invisible force, and it shot like an arrow
to the finishing-line.

The crowd roared, and the herald proclaimed Cloanthus
the winner. Aeneas stepped forward to present the prizes.
Cloanthus was crowned with bay leaves and received a
beautiful cloak of gold thread patterned in purple. Mnestheus, in second place, was cheered heartily as he was
presented with a handsome breast-plate of gold chain-mail.
Gyas was handed a set of carved bowls in copper and
silver. As the three bore off their prizes amid general

applause, the unfortunate Sergestus finally succeeded in bringing his crippled ship to harbour, with many oars missing, and many broken. The spectators laughed at this inglorious arrival, but Aeneas, pleased that no one had been hurt, came forward to greet Sergestus and gave him a slave-girl as his prize.

Athletic events were announced. They were to be held in a nearby plain, where wooded banks formed a natural stadium. For the running-race competitors came flocking from all parts of the crowd, local men as well as Trojans, all the more when Aeneas declared that everyone who entered would receive a prize. "The winner," he continued, "will get this splendid horse. The second prize is a jewelled quiver filled with arrows, and the third this fine helmet, captured from the Greeks in Troy."

Among the eager runners at the starting-line were two friends, Euryalus and Nisus. As soon as the signal was given, Nisus sped like the wind ahead of all the others. The race was as good as won, when all of a sudden he trod in a mess of blood and dung left from the recent sacrifice, slid helplessly, and fell flat on his face. The spectators gasped. Nisus half-rose, spattered with blood and dirt, saw that his friend Euryalus was in third place, and flung himself bodily in front of the second runner, a man called Salius. Salius tripped and fell, and Euryalus dashed past him to win the race. The crowd cheered loudly; for the handsome Euryalus was a popular winner. Salius began to object furiously, gesticulating at the judges and shouting that he had been the victim of foul play. His friends took up the cry, "Foul! Foul! Salius! We want Salius!" The majority, however, continued to support Euryalus, and began to chant his name and stamp their feet in rhythm.

The judges were looking anxiously at Aeneas. As he was seen to rise, the spectators stopped shouting and waited to hear his verdict. There was a tense pause. "The order cannot be changed," announced Aeneas. "Euryalus was first. Bad luck, Salius. But here, as a personal gift from me, take this lionskin. I hate to see a good friend disappointed."

Salius stammered his thanks, and his friends cheered. Nisus, however, exclaimed hotly, "What about me? I would have won easily if I hadn't slipped. Look at me — don't I deserve a prize?" Some of the spectators laughed at the bold youth, still covered in mud and filth from his fall. Aeneas laughed too, but then patted Nisus on the back in fatherly fashion and presented him with a valuable shield.

The boxing match was next. Aeneas described the prizes: a bullock all decorated with garlands and gilded horns for the winner, a consolation prize of sword and helmet for the loser. At once a powerful young champion called Dares stepped forward. As his skill and strength were well known, there was no rush of challengers. Dares grinned around at the murmuring crowd, flexing his brawny arms, and then laid his hand on the bullock. "I claim the prize!" he roared.

Acestes, as host, felt obliged to supply a match for the visiting champion. He nudged his neighbour, a veteran boxer named Entellus, and urged him to remember his reputation. "I'm not the young hero I was," protested Entellus. "The years have slowed me down. There was a time when I wore gloves seven hides think, weighted with iron and lead. Here they are — the very gloves that stood up to Hercules! Take a good look at them, Dares!

Frightening, eh?" He flung the massive objects into the arena, and pulled himself to his feet. "Come on then, since the younger generation has lost its nerve, I'll fight you man to man, if someone will provide us both with ordinary gloves."

Two pairs of gloves, identical in weight and thickness, were immediately supplied. The spectators settled back to watch, comparing Dares' youth and strength with Entellus' huge, knotted muscles and experienced air.

Dares attacked fiercely, jabbing rapidly at his opponent from every angle. Entellus was soon struggling for breath, but managed, by skilful ducking and weaving, to avoid most of the blows. At last he attempted a heavy punch, missed, lost his balance, and collapsed in a grunting heap. Acestes helped him to rise. No one had laughed, but Entellus' pride was hurt, and he flung himself into a determined pounding of his opponent. Now it was Dares who had to give ground. Thick and fast the blows came, until it seemed that Entellus would not stop till he had knocked the young man senseless.

"Stop the fight!" It was Aeneas' voice. Dares was led away, spitting blood and loose teeth from his torn lips, dizzy and punch-drunk. The garlanded bullock was awarded to the veteran Entellus, who immediately slaughtered it, crushing its skull with one terrific blow of his fist between the horns.

For the archery contest, Aeneas himself devised the target: in the middle of the arena a ship's mast was erected; almost at its top a living dove was tied to it with a cord. There were four competitors, the last being old Acestes. The first archer took aim and shot; his arrow came close to the dove, and stuck fast in the wooden mast by its foot.

The poor creature flapped its wings pitifully. The second contestant was that same Mnestheus who had almost won the boat-race. Eager for a victory this time, he took careful aim. His shaft missed the bird, but cut cleanly through the cord that bound it. The startled dove made off at once for the sky and freedom, but not soon enough. The third archer was ready, bow bent. He let fly, and the bird tumbled to the earth, spitted on the arrow. Acestes was left with no target to aim at, but he was determined to prove himself as fit as the young men. He shot high into the open sky. The arrow flashed from the bow, soared into the clouds, then caught fire and vanished in a streak of flame.

There was no mistaking an omen from the gods. Aeneas embraced his old friend and bestowed on him the first prize, an engraved bowl that had belonged to Anchises, and crowned him with the wreath of victory. No one disputed the award, and the other contestants accepted the lesser prizes cheerfully.

Now the crowd was ordered back to leave a larger area clear. Aeneas waved his hand, a fanfare sounded, and young Iulus rode into the arena at the head of a parade of noble Trojan boys, all proudly mounted, with garlands on their heads and polished weapons in their hands. Their leader was riding the horse Dido had given him in Carthage, and was the best-looking of them all.

The boys trotted slowly around the edge of the arena, while the spectators applauded each one warmly, and made fond comments on family likenesses. Then they prepared to admire the display for which the boys had practised so intently.

During all the excitement of the games, none of the men

had given a thought to the Trojan women who were sitting in a disconsolate group on the shore by the ships. The years of homeless wandering had tired them thoroughly, and they were sick at the thought of putting to sea yet again.

They could not know that they were being observed. For some time Juno had been watching for an opportunity to strike again at the Trojan expedition. Choosing her moment, she sent her servant Iris on a spiteful errand.

As soon as Iris touched the shore, she shed her divine appearance and kicked aside the rainbow trail that always marked her path. In a single instant she was disguised as an elderly and respected Trojan matron called Beroe. Taking her place among the grumbling women, she spoke in complaining tones, "I don't see why we should put up with this! Enough is enough! Seven years of nothing but trouble, ever since we left Troy. I tell you, none of us is going to live to see Italy." The other women nodded and muttered indignantly in agreement. "If it's a settlement we're looking for," went on the supposed Beroe, "just what is wrong with this place here? The people are suitable; Acestes is our own relative; I say it's good enough for me! Let's insist on staying here."

"I couldn't agree more, Beroe," said a stout matron, firmly folding her arms. "I think we should go and talk some commonsense into those men. They're living in a dream-world."

"Talking won't do any good," the disguised goddess asserted. "We must show them some action! I know what to do — I had a dream last night about poor Cassandra: she was waving a torch and saying, 'Make this your home!'

Look, ladies, this is our chance! Let's burn those wretched ships! Follow me!"

The astounded women saw the dignified figure of Beroe suddenly jump up, snatch a firebrand from a nearby altar, and with unbelievable strength hurl the leaping flame at the ships. There was a shriek — and then the oldest of the women screamed, "That's not Beroe! She's lying sick in bed! Look at those blazing eyes — it's a goddess, I tell you!" At this the figure of Beroe laughed maliciously, and before their terrified gaze, turned into a radiant, youthful maiden. Still laughing, Iris shot up into the clouds, leaving her unmistakable rainbow trail.

Now the Trojan women lost all control of their shaken wits. Shocked into a state of frenzy, they raced from altar to altar, seizing the torches and flinging them at the ships. The wild madness grew; cackling and screaming, they piled twigs and branches over the benches, the rigging and the tar-smeared decks.

"Fire! Fire!" A breathless messenger brought the alarm to the sportsground, where the boys' cavalry parade was still in progress. "The women have gone mad! They're burning the ships!"

At once Iulus wheeled his horse, and galloped at full speed to the beach. "Stop!" he cried, "You're burning our future! Listen to me — I'm Ascanius, your prince!" In despair he threw his helmet at the hysterical band. The arrival of Aeneas and a crowd of Trojan and Sicilian men broke the spell. With a final howl of frenzy, the women scattered and ran into the wood.

Buckets were snatched from the farthest ships, where the fire had not yet spread. Salt water was passed from hand to hand and flung on the blazing timber, but the fire had already eaten into the holds and the smouldering tar only hissed in menace when the water touched it.

Aeneas turned his eyes to the sky. "Almighty Jupiter," he prayed, "if we have been true to you, then help us now, or send us a quick death."

A blast of thunder answered him. Black clouds rolled over the clear sky, and a deluge of rain drenched the crowd on the shore, extinguishing the smouldering fires. All but four of the ships were saved.

Delighted by the miracle, the Trojans relaxed into a happy, exuberant mood, ready to trust in the gods, their leader and their destiny. But Aeneas himself retired to his quarters, and summoned his senior officers to a council. "How long can I try the patience of these people?" he was thinking. "Do I have the right to draw them over the sea against their will?"

The officers arrived. Without waiting for Aeneas to open the council, an elderly captain called Nautes addressed him. "Sir, forgive me for speaking first, but I think I understand the present problem. There is no point in a half-hearted expedition to Italy. Now this land of Sicily, it's not so bad. Acestes is our kinsman and . . ."

"Are you suggesting that we give up and stay here?" Aeneas faced him with angry eyes.

"No, no, my lord," said Nautes, "just hear me out. Why not offer a settlement here to those who would prefer it? Those who are tired, faint-hearted, sick of adventures — we don't want them in Italy any more than they want to come. We need to cut down our numbers, anyway, since we have lost four ships. Acestes would co-operate, I feel sure, especially if we named the settlement after him."

The words of Nautes seemed good sense, but Aeneas

could not pronounce a decision at once. He wandered away by himself to think. Darkness came. As he sat alone by the sea, wrestling with his worries, a phantom glided through the silent air, and spoke to him in the voice of his father, Anchises: "Dear son, Jupiter has sent me to help you. Nautes spoke good advice. Take only a picked band of your bravest young men to Italy. The natives there are fierce, and you will have to meet them in battle."

Aeneas breathed his relief and thanks. But the phantom had more to say: "When you reach the shores of Italy, my son, seek out the Sibyl. She will lead you through the dark kingdom of the dead, through the deep haunts of Pluto's kingdom, to visit me in the Land of the Blessed. There I will show you the future of your race. I feel the touch of day; I must return. Do not fail me, Aeneas." The vision faded into the chill air of dawn.

Acestes agreed readily to Aeneas' proposals. The arrangements were quickly made: the people were divided according to their wishes, and Aeneas marked out the boundaries of the new city and consecrated shrines to Venus and to the memory of Anchises.

Only when the moment of parting came did the Trojans realise that they had each made a binding decision. Some of the women who had been loudest in their abuse of the sea now sobbed and begged not to be left behind. Aeneas did his best to console them, reminding them that Acestes was their cousin, and that they would be living among friends.

The ships were hauled to the water; Aeneas was the last to board; the rowers were fresh and eager.

In the domain of the gods, Venus was anxiously pleading with Neptune, the ruler of the seas. "Remember how once before Juno dared to interfere with your kingdom? All I ask now is a safe passage for my son, Aeneas, and his people to the shores of Italy."

In his deep, rolling voice, Neptune pronounced, "What you ask is only proper, and I shall grant your request. Aeneas will reach his Italian harbour safely. I claim only one life in return for many."

One life? Aeneas had no thought of danger. The breeze was strong. The sails filled out contentedly on all the ships, as they moved in convoy following the course steered by Palinurus. When the sun set, all the rowers rested, but Palinurus kept steady watch, his hand on the tiller of the flagship. The night was peaceful. Palinurus watched the stars, felt the gentle rocking of the deck, and heard a low, enticing voice, "Sleep, Palinurus," it said, "your eyes are heavy. Sleep!"

"No!" Palinurus cried to the empty air. "How can I sleep on duty? Aeneas needs my skill. The sea is treacherous!"

What happened then Palinurus never knew. A slumber he could not resist came over him; still clinging to the tiller he was tipped overboard. No one heard the crack of the timber as it was wrenched away.

The unusual lurching of the ship roused Aeneas, and brought him to the afterdeck. The broken tiller told him enough. "Palinurus," he groaned, "why did you trust the sea?" The ship glided on, while Aeneas took over as helmsman, and wept for his loyal friend, now a nameless body on some unknown shore.

VI Aeneas in the Land of the Dead

AENEAS wept for his friend, Palinurus, beside the broken tiller, but he held the ship on course. Neptune kept his promise to Venus, and in return for Palinurus' life brought the Trojans to their goal. Straight ahead, the hills of Italy stood grey against the dawn. Aeneas murmured a prayer of thanks, and shouted "Land! Land ahead!"

Very soon excited Trojans were tumbling out onto the welcoming shore. Like children they ran this way and that, exclaiming when they found running streams, or glimpsed forest animals, or spied the precious flintstones they needed for making fire.

Aeneas left them to explore. True to his father's command, he made his way at once to the temple of Apollo where, at the entrance to a black and bottomless cave, the Sibyl guarded her frightening secrets. The temple was a fine building, adorned with carved scenes from ancient tales, but Aeneas could not stop for long to admire it. "Slay seven bullocks and seven sheep, all perfect and unblemished − before you enter this holy place," came a command from within. As soon as the sacrifice had been performed, the Sibyl appeared and beckoned. An aged, shrivelled creature with reddened eyes, she seemed born of shadows and dank places.

75

Aeneas followed her to the inner part of the temple. There he found himself in a huge cave, in which the walls and vaulted roof were pitted with a hundred black and gaping mouths. "The god! I feel the god!" the Sibyl screamed. Her hair flew wildly about her head, she gasped for breath and her face turned livid. In a voice far different from her former rasping whine, she proclaimed, "Speak now, Aeneas of Troy! Make your prayer. So may you open the lips of the god and learn your fate."

Chilled and shivering with awe, Aeneas could only whisper, "Apollo, you have always been good to us. In Troy your hand guided the fatal arrow, when Paris shot the hateful Achilles dead. Be good to us, now that we are in Italy at last. O you gods and goddesses who stood against Troy's ancient city, set aside your malice, and spare us in this new land." He paused, shuddering at memories of Troy. "Holy priestess," he now addressed the Sibyl, "I ask for a safe home in Italy for my people and our home-gods. Speak, I pray, gracious lady."

The Sibyl was still struggling to control the powerful force that was exhausting her; she rocked from side to side, her face twisted with frenzy. When at last she opened her lips to speak, a hundred voices boomed at once from the hundred stony mouths, hurling the words across the cavern, until Aeneas was spinning in a whirl of clashing sound: "The dangers of the sea are past; the dangers of the land await you. You will come to the soil of Latium, children of Troy, but you will not be glad. I see the land bristling with war, the Tiber flowing with blood. Another Achilles is waiting to savage you. Juno is still your foe. Many deaths are caused by a foreign marriage. But be bold, Aeneas, wherever fortune takes you. Seek friends among the Greeks, and, whatever losses you may suffer, do not weaken."

As the re-echoing voices ceased, the Sibyl grew calmer, and finally her frenzy passed away. Then Aeneas addressed her again, "Lady, I have one more request, a serious one. They say that this is the entrance to the Underworld. I wish to travel to that place of death to visit my father, noble Anchises. I carried him from the flames of Troy; he was my guide and inspiration for so many years, but then the gods took him from me. In visions and dreams he has commanded me to make this journey. Please, holy priestess, help us to meet once more. I would not be the first − I have heard stories of Orpheus and Hercules and Theseus, all heroes who visited Pluto's kingdom while still alive. My right is no less than theirs: I, too, am born of the gods."

The Sibyl answered with a sad smile, "It is easy to reach the Land of Death, Aeneas of Troy, but steep and hard is the journey back to the light. Listen now. Search in the woods for a tree that bears a single golden bough. If the gods are with you in this venture, you will find the bough and pluck it easily from the tree. It will be a token, a passport through the Underworld, a tribute to Pluto's queen. Two further tasks − give solemn burial to your friend who, at this very moment, lies dead upon the shore, and sacrifice black sheep to the powers of the lower world. Then come."

Sick with worry, Aeneas made a speedy return to the ships. He soon saw the truth of the Sibyl's words. A circle of tearful Trojans surrounded the lifeless form of brave Misenus, a man who had fought side-by-side with Hector in Troy. Aeneas looked long at his friend's body and, biting back his sorrow, said, "Poor Misenus! We will always remember how bravely he blew his trumpet on the plains of Troy. Come, friends, let us give him the honour he deserves." Following their leader's example, the Trojans began to fell trees for a funeral pyre. Reverently they set out oil and incense, and dressed the dead warrior in polished armour.

"Misenus proved the Sibyl true," Aeneas said to himself, "I must trust her words, and search for the golden bough that she described. I only wish it could appear before me this instant." His musing was interrupted by a sudden fluttering and cooing. Two doves had landed on the ground in front of him. He smiled to see them, for doves were the favourite birds of his mother, the goddess Venus. As he watched, the doves rose into the air again, calling insistently. They flew a little way further into the wood, and landed on a tall tree. Aeneas gazed after them, and then exclaimed in wonder, for amid the dark leaves was an unmistakable glimmer of gold. One quick wrench, and the magic bough was in his hand.

The Sibyl was waiting for his return. Without a word she pointed to an opening in the rock, so deep, so high and, somehow, so pitiless, that it drained the surrounding scene of all movement and life. No birds flew near that place, where withered leaves drifted onto the stagnant lake, and the stench of decay waited for a breeze that never blew.

Together, the Sibyl and Aeneas made sacrifices to the gods of the Underworld, to Hecate, the witch-queen, to Night and Earth, to Pluto, king of the dead, and Proserpina, his bride. All night they performed the rites, offering black bullocks, a lamb with black fleece, and a barren cow. At dawn, when the air was chill and the altar-fires were dying to a glow, they felt the ground shake with the witch-queen's tread, and heard the eerie howling of her dogs.

"Stand back, stand back," the Sibyl pronounced solemnly, "unless you share this mystery! Draw your sword, Aeneas, and prove your courage!" She sank into the darkness of the cave; without hesitation the hero followed.

The path was dim and shadowy; strange patterns flickered back and forth in a pale, joyless dance; their footsteps echoed in the empty chambers. They felt presences they could not see: the spirits of Grief, Disease, Old Age, Fear, Hunger and Poverty, Death and its brother Sleep, mad Passion, and deadly War — figures that leered at them through the shadows.

As the path opened out, a huge tree loomed before them, its branches crammed with deceiving dreams. A frightful hissing and screeching came from a number of vaults around the tree. From den after den a fearsome creature lunged: a Centaur, human face grinning, horse-tail swishing, the six-headed Scylla, Chimaera, the fire-breathing lion-goat-dragon, the snake-haired Gorgon, and a nameless, three-bodied Thing.

"Put away your sword, Aeneas," the Sibyl urged the trembling hero, "these monsters were all killed long ago; they are harmless to us now."

The path was becoming slippery underfoot. Groping for the rocky wall, Aeneas' fingers touched a slimy dampness. He became aware of a sound of slow bubbling not far ahead. "We are near the dismal marsh of the Styx," the Sibyl said. "Soon we shall see the place of crossing."

Aeneas had no need to ask her to explain, for they had arrived at the bank of the most unlovely river he had ever

seen. Its sluggish current gurgled through the reeds that
bristled across its surface, clotted with stinking mud. The
bank was thronged with human shapes, all stretching out
their arms and moaning pitifully — children, mothers,
warriors, brides, every age and type of the human race was
represented there.

"What do they want? Why do they sound so desperate?"
Aeneas asked.

"They are the souls of the dead whose bodies lie unburied," the Sibyl answered. "They are not allowed to
cross the river Styx until one hundred years have passed,
but must haunt this cheerless bank. That boat you see
there is the only means of crossing, and the boatman is
Charon, who selects those who may lawfully pass."

Now Aeneas could see that a dingy, rust-coloured punt
with ragged sails lay alongside the bank; within it stood an
aged boatman, with filthy, matted beard and blazing eyes.
Sternly he waved back the horde of imploring spirits, and
chose one or two who climbed thankfully aboard.

"Palinurus," Aeneas suddenly cried out, "Oh, tell me,
what has become of you?"

The drifting shade that had once been the Trojan steersman turned, and recognised his captain. "Is it really you,
sir, alive in this hellish place? Oh, help me to find rest! I
was washed overboard, tiller and all, by a monstrous wave.
I swam to shore, worried out of my mind about the ship,
only to be butchered by natives as soon as I touched land.
Sir, the gods must be helping you to make this dreaded
journey — put in a word for me! Take me with you across
the river!"

Before Aeneas could reply to his wretched friend, the
Sibyl interposed, "How dare you try to break the eternal

laws of the gods? No unburied soul may cross the Styx, however much it may plead. But rest assured, good man, your body will be honoured with a fitting tomb, and the region around it will bear your name."

An aged grating voice called from the boat, "Who comes to my river in arms? This land is for the dead, for shades and sleep, not for so-called heroes who come to plunder!"

"No fear of plunder," answered the Sibyl, "We mean no harm. This is Aeneas of Troy, true of heart and staunch in war, who comes to pay respect to his honoured father. See, we bring a token." She pulled the golden bough from the folds of her robe.

Charon said no more. Sweeping the moaning ghosts from his boat, he allowed Aeneas and the Sibyl to climb aboard, shaking his head ruefully as the boat creaked and dipped under the unusual weight.

Hardly had they stepped onto the opposite bank when a tremendous barking broke out. Cerberus, Pluto's enormous watch-dog, crouched in its lair, its three mouths showing three sets of wicked fangs. The Sibyl simply tossed it a biscuit soaked in a sleeping-potion, and in a moment, the creature lay prone on the floor, its three necks splayed out in a drugged slumber.

Aeneas breathed hard in relief: "Where are we now? Surely that can't be a baby crying?"

"Not just one baby," the Sibyl replied. "Here are the souls of all the infants who die at birth. Listen to them, doomed to cry for their mothers to the end of time."

Aeneas could not stop to comment; other extraordinary sights and sounds were crowding upon him. "What is this court-room here?"

"These are new trials for those unjustly condemned to

death. Those fretting souls you see over there are suicides. And now, look there, the Fields of Sorrow, the haunt of those who died for love."

Aeneas stared in the direction of the Sibyl's pointing hand, and broke into a run. "Dido!" he cried after a figure straying through the trees. "Dido, wait! I swear I did not want to leave! The gods, the same gods who made me come to this dreaded place forced me to leave you. How could I think that you would . . . Don't turn away!" She had stopped, her eyes on the ground, showing no sign of recognition. Now she turned and vanished into the wood, where the ghost of her husband Sychaeus was waiting to comfort her. Aeneas stood stiff with hopeless longing and unspeakable grief.

The path led on. They came to the most distant fields of the region, set apart for warriors who had met a noble death. Immediately, Aeneas was the centre of a jostling swarm of eager ghosts. Trojan after Trojan he greeted, as they thrust their fleshless hands at him, clamouring in thin, wavering voices. In a silent, separate group, the Greek warriors watched the scene of reunion. As Aeneas drew near them, some turned and fled in terror, while others opened their mouths to roar a war-cry that came out faint and distant.

Among the Trojans Aeneas noticed one who did not press forward, but kept his distance. His body showed the marks of dreadful wounds, and when he moved, his face revealed the most hideous and pitiful disfigurement. For all this, he was recognizable. Aeneas stared in horror at the mangled features of Deiphobus, son of Priam, one of great Hector's brothers. "Who did this to you, Deiphobus?"

Aeneas said at last. "Who in all the world could hate you so much?"

"My wife, Aeneas, that wonderful Helen I married after Paris was killed. You probably know that she betrayed us, signalling to the Greek fleet from our towers, dancing around the wooden horse with a blazing firebrand. I was asleep that happy night, alone in our bed; she hid my weapons, and opened the door to that blustering fool Menelaus, her first husband. Ulysses was with him: you can see what they did then. But enough about me; what brings you to this place?"

They could have talked for hours, but the Sibyl urged Aeneas to hurry on. "It is nearly night; we have no time to spare."

Before them the path divided. Aeneas paused, and looked to the priestess for guidance. "We take the road on the right," she said, "which leads to the Fields of Blessed Happiness, called Elysium. The left road leads to Tartarus, the place of torment and damnation."

As they went on, the Sibyl described to Aeneas the horrible fate of those condemned to suffer for their sins in Tartarus. They were surrounded by a triple wall and moat of fire; the only entrance was a gate so strong that even the gods could not break it down. The place itself was an enormous pit, twice as deep as Mount Olympus was high. For each sinner the gods had devised a separate form of torture: one lay spreadeagled over nine acres, his innards forever being torn by a vulture; another rolled a huge boulder uphill but it always slipped back; one starved in agony before tables of delicious food; another spun round and round, tied to a whirling wheel of fire.

This grim catalogue of tortures lasted them to the very

gates of Pluto's palace, where Aeneas set down the golden bough as an offering to Proserpina, queen of the Underworld. Then they entered the Fields of Happiness.

The first thing Aeneas noticed was the light. All their journey, up to this point, had taken place in semi-darkness, as one might expect in a place cut off from the sun. But Elysium was a land of miracles: it had its own sky, where a sun shone by day and stars sparkled by night. Rich, rolling grasslands were bounded by clear rivers and groves of shady trees. Sleek horses, free of harness, grazed peacefully. This was the home of those who had served their country well by their courage, their conduct, or their talents, or those who were fondly remembered for their good deeds. Here they were free to play games, and sing, and listen to music and poetry.

Aeneas found his father in a deep, lush valley, counting over a long procession of spirits not yet born: these were his descendants, one day to be the Roman race. As soon as Anchises saw Aeneas, he left the task and stretched out his arms to his son, tears rolling down his faded cheeks.

"I knew you would be true, Aeneas. I know you would come at last, daring even the most dreaded of all journeys to visit me. Let me look at you properly. I have been so worried about you, my son, especially when you were in Carthage."

Aeneas, sobbing freely, tried three times to hug his father. But Anchises belonged now to the world of dreams and shadows; his spirit glided like a puff of wind through the clutching arms of his son.

For a while they simply walked and talked, Aeneas asking many questions about Elysium, and particularly the thousands of spirits who clustered like bees about the banks of a river. His father explained that these were souls about to be re-born into the world above. "All of us bear an immortal spark within us, a force of eternal fire that is Life and Soul and Mind. When we die, our earthly bodies rot away but our spirits escape. Here in the lower world our souls are cleansed of sin. At last, a few of us, the lucky ones, are allowed to enter this happy place. The river is called Lethe; the crowds you see on its banks have waited for a thousand years. One sip of Lethe's water washes away all memories, and makes them ready for another life."

Anchises paused to allow Aeneas to digest what he had heard, and then beckoned him to a grassy bank. From this point they could observe a long procession passing below.

"Listen and watch with close attention, my son," Anchises began, "for these are the great men of Trojan blood, your descendants, who will one day rule the world. You will marry an Italian princess, Lavinia by name, and that young man who leads the parade is your youngest son — look at him, Aeneas. His name is Silvius, father of the royal dynasty of Alba Longa, a new city founded by your children. The next in line are his successors, king after noble king. Now do you see the man with two plumes on his helmet? Take good note of him. His mother is a princess of Alba Longa, his father none less than the god Mars. His name is Romulus, who shall build a city on seven hills, and call it Rome.

"Now turn, Aeneas, and look this way. These are the heroes of Rome, your Rome. And this one here is the greatest of all, the man whose rule will be a Golden Age, whose power will stretch to the ends of the earth — Augustus Caesar, divine in blood.

"These are the kings of infant Rome, the hated Tarquins, a tyrant family who will be driven out of your city by this man, Brutus, founder of the republic and champion of free government. See, a line of valiant warriors! Their deeds of bravery will shine throughout the world. But look, Caesar and Pompey, Romans both, facing each other with hostile swords. No, children of mine: don't tear your country apart with civil wars! Aeneas, look at these, their names shall be the building-blocks of history — Cato, the Gracchi, the Scipios, and Quintus Fabius, known as the Delayer."

Anchises now turned to his son, placed his shadowy hands about Aeneas' shoulders, and looked him full in the face. "You are a Roman. You must remember the noble gift that is yours alone. Not art, nor literature, nor science, but government! Spare the conquered, crush the proud; for your task it is to tame the world and bring it peaceful rule."

It was nearly time to part. They wandered for a little while longer around the green fields of Elysium, Anchises now speaking of the dangers that Italy would bring to his son. He described the city of King Latinus, and explained what steps Aeneas should take to make his settlement successful.

They were drawing near the two gates that lead out from the Underworld. They are known as the Gates of Sleep, one made of horn, the other of ivory. Anchises waved his son and the Sibyl through the portals of the ivory gate, and stood looking after them.

Aeneas hurried back to his ships, and the Trojans sailed northwards along the coast to seek the mouth of the river Tiber, and the land of Latium.

VII   The Trojans Come to Latium

NOT far from the mouth of the River Tiber the Laurentes lived in a walled city, peaceful, prosperous and strong. They were ruled by old King Latinus, whose word was respected throughout that part of Italy known as Latium. King Latinus was descended, they said, from the ancient god Saturn, father of Jupiter, for Saturn had once lived in that fertile and blessed country.

The king had devoted his life to the city and its people, and it was his dearest wish to leave his kingdom to a worthy successor. He had only one child, a daughter called Lavinia. Because Lavinia's husband would one day become king of the Laurentes, many local chieftains were eager to marry her. Lavinia herself was content to leave the choice of a suitable husband to her parents. King Latinus had not yet made a final decision, but his wife, Amata, was very clear in her views. She strongly favoured a relation of hers, Turnus, a proud young chieftain of the Rutulian tribe, and did all she could to persuade her husband to accept him.

Now in the central courtyard of the palace grew an ancient laurel tree, much treasured by the king, who had named his people "Laurentes" in its honour. Near the tree were altars to the gods, where the king and his household would gather to perform sacrifices and recite prayers.

It was during a ceremony of this kind that a miracle occurred. A large swarm of bees suddenly flew into the courtyard and clustered among the leaves of the laurel tree, buzzing loudly and insistently. At this unusual sight a priest exclaimed, "A sign from heaven! These bees foretell a swarm of strangers, settling in the heart of this land!" Before the king could answer, there was a shriek from the princess. Lavinia was standing in a shower of sparks; her hair was ablaze, and the jewelled crown she wore encircled her head with flame. And yet, despite this, she remained unharmed.

The king, greatly alarmed, hurried to a secret grove in the forest, a place set apart for the worship of his own father, Faunus, a god of the Italian countryside. Latinus made the ritual offerings, and waited. From the depths of the wood he heard a deep, commanding voice: "Listen and obey, my son. Do not give your child Lavinia to any man of Latium; no Latin is destined to be her husband. Expect a suitor from a foreign land; him she must marry, and their children will be a race famous for all time. They will rule the earth in glory from ocean to ocean."

King Latinus returned to his palace, and, despite his wife's urgent pleading, postponed the choice of a husband for his daughter. Turnus returned to his own people, disappointed and impatient, for he had come to look upon Lavinia as his promised bride.

Meanwhile the Trojans, knowing little of Latium and its inhabitants, were pulling in to the mouth of the river Tiber. In the early-morning sunlight the landing-place looked perfect – a forest close to the shore, thickly-wooded and sparkling with bird-song; and through the mass of green wound the river, its yellowish stream spreading out to embrace the Trojan ships. Iulus remarked that it was as though the Tiber flowed out to welcome them.

Their first meal in the new land was simple. Lying in the soft, shaded grass, they piled fresh fruit onto large, flat loaves that were to serve as plates, table-linen, and tables. After eating the fruit, they finished off their meal with the bread, too hungry to leave a morsel uneaten.

"Chewing up the dining-tables," said Iulus, chuckling at his own wit. The Trojans laughed, but Aeneas did not join in. Achates, noticing his friend's frown of concentration, asked, "Is there something wrong?"

"No, nothing wrong. This is a sign from the gods. It is time to begin our settlement. My father Anchises once told me, long ago, that when we reached our promised land we would set about chewing our tables."

"I'm sure I have heard those words somewhere, myself," Achates said and, after a moment's thought: "Of course. Don't you remember the curse Celaeno, the Harpy, screamed at us? Her very words were, 'You will be forced to chew your own tables!' Well, Prince Ascanius is right — here we are chewing our tables. So much for her terrible curse on our settlement!"

Next morning Aeneas sent scouts to explore the country-side. They reported on the direction of the river, the position of the various villages, the name and location of the chief city. "Now we must make formal contact," Aeneas pronounced. "One hundred of you shall act as our ambassadors; Ilioneus is to be in charge. You will carry olive boughs as a symbol of peace, and take gifts for the king. Meanwhile the rest of us will pitch camp here — our first settlement in Italy. May the gods look on it with favour!"

King Latinus received the Trojan deputation in his huge throne-room. The walls were lined with trophies − shields, swords, axes, helmets, even chariots and the prows of ships, all captured from defeated enemies. Statues of gods and heroes gazed down at the newcomers as they stared at so much unexpected grandeur.

"Come, friends," King Latinus began, "you say you are Trojans? Then you are not completely strange to our land. I have heard tales of your ancestor, Dardanus, who was born here in Italy. What has brought you so far? Did you lose your course at sea? Has some disaster driven you to our shore?"

The moment had come for Ilioneus to speak. He chose his words carefully, knowing how much depended on the impression he made: "Great king, our mother city, Troy, once the centre of a mighty nation, no longer exists. It perished in a terrible war with the Greeks, a war in which the heavenly gods themselves took their part. I'm sure you've heard the story, for by now it has reached the ends of the earth.

"Those of us who have journeyed to this western land have been following the command of Jupiter himself. Our leader is Aeneas, son of Venus and royal Anchises of Troy. We were guided by Apollo's oracles to make for this land, once the home of our founder, Dardanus, to end here our years of wandering and establish a new settlement for our weary people. We come in peace. And we ask of you, your majesty, no more than a plot of land so that we may carry out the decrees of fate. As a token of friendship we offer you these gifts."

Ilioneus signed to some of the Trojans, who placed
before the king priceless relics rescued from Troy – King
Priam's own crown, sceptre and ceremonial robe, and a
gold dish used by Anchises for making sacred offerings
to the gods.

There was a long silence. King Latinus did not appear
much interested in the gifts, but sat staring at the floor,
lost in thought. A few of the Trojans exchanged uneasy
glances.

"May the gods bless this beginning," the king's voice
suddenly boomed through the hall. He rose and beckoned
to the startled Ilioneus. "Tell your leader that I grant his
request, but I wish him to appear before me in person. I
am delighted to greet him, and not only as an ally. I have a
daughter, Lavinia, who, it is foretold, must marry a foreign
suitor. Your prince Aeneas must surely be the man!"

No rules of etiquette could suppress the excitement of
the Trojan contingent and, no less, of the king's own
courtiers. The murmuring grew to a babbling, but the king
did not seem affronted. Smiling broadly, he shook hands
with Ilioneus, and ordered gifts for all the embassy:
a splendid war-horse decked out in gold harness for each of
the hundred men, and for Aeneas himself, a chariot drawn
by two immortal, fire-breathing steeds, bred in the Sun-
god's magical stables.

The success of the embassy delighted Aeneas. Over and
over Ilioneus had to repeat the king's words, and each time
the Trojans cheered and applauded. Aeneas decided to
visit the Laurentes the following morning, and set
his servants to polishing his armour and laying out his
finest clothes.

He never gave a thought to Juno. Always watchful,

always bitter, the queen of the gods had observed the happy landing, and the joyful spirits of the Trojans in their camp. "This time I will succeed!" she swore. "Those Trojans have escaped every trap I set, in Troy, Carthage, Sicily and on the stormy seas. They laugh at me; they mock my vengeance! Very well, if my heavenly power is too weak, I'll use the forces of hell! If I can't prevent this settlement, if Aeneas must marry this Latin bride, then at least I will mark these happy events with bloodshed, havoc and war!" Juno plunged down to the earth, and summoned, from the black depths of the Underworld, a screaming, spitting creature of evil.

Allecto was the creature's name. She was one of the Furies, a loathsome sisterhood born of Night, whose bluish hair was intertwined with venomous snakes, and whose business was violence and bloody destruction.

"Do this for me!" Juno urged, though even her spiteful nature shrank from the hideous demon before her. "Shatter the peace in Latium! You know a thousand ways of stirring up hatred and quarrels. I need your skill. Sow strife in Italy, and make the Trojans bleed!"

As the goddess spoke, Allecto's fangs grinned from her jaws. The task pleased her. Swooping invisible into King Latinus' palace, she hovered about windows and doorways, waiting for a chance. She listened intently as Queen Amata pleaded with her husband to bestow his daughter's hand on Turnus, and she followed the disappointed mother as she retired weeping at the king's stubborn refusal.

The Fury saw her chance. She plucked a hissing snake from her hair and cast it at the Queen. The creature glided over Amata's skin, and began to work its venom deep into her heart. The queen sighed and rose. She would try once more to persuade her husband.

"What is it now, my dear?" the king asked, as patiently as he could.

"Our daughter's marriage. Now, don't groan at me like that. Believe me, I only want the best for her."

"Haven't we discussed this already, Amata? I have given you my answer."

"You haven't thought about it properly," the queen retorted. "You say Lavinia must marry a foreigner – that such is the will of the gods. Do you seriously think the gods intend our daughter to marry an outcast, a landless beggar? You have heard the story of Paris – don't you see, these Trojans are well-known for stealing women and carrying them off across the sea. How do you know they mean to settle here in Italy? We may never see Lavinia again!"

"Enough, woman!" groaned the king, putting his hands over his ears. "What do you know of the gods' will?"

"I know that the gods often speak in riddles, and mislead men. A foreigner? What is a foreigner? Someone from another city. Turnus is a Rutulian, not one of us. In fact, if you go back in history, his family is Greek, an old Mycenaean race. That's 'foreign' enough to satisfy the oracle."

"Stop!" The king had risen now. Exasperation had turned to anger. "Not another word! I am still king of the Laurentes. Woman, attend to your household!"

Amata fled. Now the poison from Allecto's snake had spread through her system, and she no longer knew what she did or where she was. She uttered a piercing howl, and, seizing a torch in each hand, began to sway and twirl like a drunken worshipper at the wine-god's orgies.

"Bacchus calls! Bacchus calls! Hail, Bacchus!" She swung the torches to and fro before the faces of her horrified ladies, until they too caught the rhythm and began to roll their eyes and lurch from side to side.

"Hail, great Bacchus!" the women cried in chorus, and, as if at a signal, plucked torches from the wall-hooks and danced after the frenzied queen. Up and down the passages swayed the maddened line, gathering more and more of the palace women. The queen's voice rose shrill above the rest. "Sing a wedding-hymn! Hail, great god Bacchus! Sing to Lavinia and noble Turnus! Sing a wedding-hymn!"

Faster and faster spun the dance. The queen caught her daughter by the arm, and wrenched her into the twirling line. "A bride!" she screamed. "A bride for Turnus! A bride for Bacchus! Hail, hail, great Bacchus!"

Into the courtyard, into the streets, into the forest they danced. The men of the city watched helpless as their wives and daughters joined the hectic band. When the last of the dancers had vanished into the woods, the men knew they could only wait till the spell subsided. It was foolish to interfere with the rites of Bacchus.

The Fury Allecto had been following the women with delight, adding her shrieks to the general din, and increasing the commotion with her evil magic. Now she saw that her work among the Laurentes was complete. At nightfall she flew to Ardea, the home of Turnus.

Turnus was asleep. Disguised as an elderly priestess of Juno, the Fury invaded the young man's dreams: "Turnus, are you sleeping while King Latinus cheats you of your promised bride? Are you a man? Will you allow Lavinia to marry a Trojan upstart? What are you waiting for? The

Trojans are at your mercy. Burn their ships, and put them to the sword! This is the will of gracious Juno."

Turnus stirred in his sleep, and murmured, "Go away, old woman; mind your own business, and leave matters of war to men!"

At this Allecto shed her disguise, and towered above the sleeping warrior, her eyes blazing red, her snaky hair writhing and rearing, a whip in one hand, a firebrand in the other: "Foolish old woman, am I? Then look again, Turnus, and tremble!" She hurled the torch deep into his heart, so that he woke in a fervour, raging for blood and revenge. In a matter of hours, the young men of Ardea were reporting for battle, echoing Turnus' vows of death to the Trojans and punishment for King Latinus.

Meanwhile Allecto had just one more visit to make. Spying on the Trojan camp, she saw young Iulus and his friends setting out for a hunt. Chattering in excitement, they began to lay snares and discuss the game. Their hounds ran barking around them. Perched in a tree, Allecto glimpsed the antlers of a handsome stag, cooling itself in the river.

The stag roaming the forest was the pet of a village girl called Silvia. Her brothers had found it as a tiny fawn. Now fully grown, still tame and very attached to its mistress, it wandered freely by day, and pawed at the door of her house every evening. All the village people knew Silvia's pet, and took care not to hunt it by mistake.

Now Allecto dropped close to the stag. It sensed her presence, and froze, quivering with terror. The Fury drew breath, and blew a long, strident blast of air. The scent of the frightened stag was borne through the forest, and reached the keen nostrils of the Trojan hounds.

In a second the dogs were yelping furiously and bounding through the trees. "A scent!" shouted Iulus, and raced in pursuit, notching his arrow as he ran. The sight of the splendid beast thrilled him with excitement. What a trophy to show his father! His aim was true. The arrow stuck fast in the animal's flank.

Crazed with pain, the stag kicked aside the attacking hounds and ran for the village. Whimpering and squealing, it pounded with its hooves on Silvia's door, and collapsed at her feet. The girls' cries brought the villagers rushing to the house. "Who did this?" demanded one of her brothers.

There was no need to search. Iulus, at the head of his band, had appeared from the woods, panting from the chase. With a roar, Silvia's brother set upon him, brandishing his woodcutter's axe.

Allecto observed the spreading brawl with glee. Seizing a shepherd's horn, she blew it again and again with all her might, so that all round the countryside men snatched up weapons and ran to answer the call to arms. The Trojans, too, heard the sound of alarm, and made for the village with all speed to rescue Iulus.

The clash of steel and roar of battle-cries were music to the Fury Allecto. She called triumphantly to Juno, "See, lady, I have done it! If you wish, I'll spread this war up and down the whole length of Italy."

"No, no," protested Juno, recoiling from the Fury's greedy lust for blood. "Enough! You have served me well. Now go back to your proper place. The rest I shall manage myself. Go quickly!" With a cackling yell that rang from the clifftops, Allecto dived, the snakes streaming from her head, straight through a cleft in the rock. A distant crash shook the base of the mountain, and she was gone.

There was strife in Latium. The angry band of villagers, carrying their dead and wounded, met Turnus and his advancing troops. Together they surrounded the palace of Latinus, and demanded an all-out war against the Trojan settlers. A crowd of citizens joined the turmoil. Their wives were still under the spell of Bacchus.

"Fight! Fight!" came the cry of the mob, pounding and battering at the palace doors. "War against the Trojans! Drive them from our shore! Turnus will lead us — we want Turnus! Turnus will fight!"

"We can't hold the doors, sir," gasped a terrified guard to King Latinus. "You must answer them."

The old king flung up his hands and appealed to the gods. "No guilt of mine! My pledge to the Trojans is firm. If Turnus sheds their blood, let the guilt be his alone." Then he added wearily, "Tell them they can do as they like."

It was enough. Juno's own hand swung back the massive iron gates that were opened only in time of war. The blare of trumpets summoned men to arms. All over Latium blacksmiths worked feverishly; horses were yoked to chariots and galloped back and forth across the plain; in the empty fields the ploughs were left to rust and rot.

Twelve powerful allies came to join Turnus, each with a menacing army. First came Mezentius, a bitter and twisted character. His own people, the Etruscans, had expelled him because of his unspeakable acts of cruelty. He was followed by Aventinus, a son of Hercules, wearing the famous lion-skin of his father. Twin brothers came next, warriors both, and a king called Caeculus, whose troops fought light-armed, with slings and slingshots of lead. Messapus, son of Neptune, brought the horses he was famous for training, and Clausus of the Sabine tribe marched after him with a huge battalion. Then came a man with good reason to hate the Trojans, Halaesus, son of the Greek king, Agamemnon, who had led the destruction of ancient Troy; Oebalus, leading troops who wore helmets made from bark; Ufens, whose tribe lived by plunder; Umbro, a magician and snake-charmer; and the handsome Virbius brought the number of allied armies to eleven.

The twelfth was a Volscian force, all cavalry. Their leader was a maiden warrior, Camilla, dressed in a royal cloak, her hair held in a clasp of gold, a quiver of arrows on her back and a spear in her hand.

Turnus himself was the tallest of all, his noble stature heightened by a helmet with three plumes, shaped like a frightening monster, which nodded and shook as he moved.

This was the army that gathered to slaughter the Trojans.

VIII Aeneas Seeks Help from Evander

NEWS came to Aeneas of the war-fever that was spreading through Latium. At first he would not believe that it was directed against himself. "It's impossible," he said to Achates, "King Latinus gave me his solemn pledge of friendship, not to mention his daughter's hand in marriage. And now, in a matter of days . . ."

"They say the old king has lost control. 'Turnus' is now the name on everyone's lips," replied Achates.

"I have no quarrel with this Turnus. We have never even met."

"I've heard he is a disappointed suitor," Achates said, with a rueful smile. "Unfortunately he has a large number of friends . . ."

"And we have none. You hardly need to remind me. I realised our position only too clearly when Ascanius nearly got himself killed in that village. He was very lucky that we heard the alarm."

Aeneas spent a restless, feverish night. Snatches of oracles haunted his memory. Past visions flooded his brain, all distorted, ugly, and mocking.

"Marry a Latin princess," the ghost of his wife Creusa seemed to whisper, and laughed.

"Italy is your promised home," taunted his family gods.

"Your city is marked by a litter of pigs," the seer Helenus was sniggering.

"War! The land bristles with war!" the Sibyl screamed, "Seek friends in a Greek city!"

"Help me, O gods!" Aeneas moaned, half-awake, half-delirious.

At last he slept. A peaceful figure glided into his dream, bearded, crowned with reeds, draped in watery robes. It spoke in a soft comforting voice: "Do not lose heart, Aeneas. This land is your home. I am the spirit of the River Tiber, giver of life to these fertile plains. On the shady bank of my stream you will find, as was foretold, a shining white sow, with thirty white piglets. It is a sign. When thirty years have passed, your son will build a city called Alba, which means 'white'.

"I will help you in your present trouble. Listen carefully. Not far from here is a settlement of Greeks, a town called Pallanteum, ruled by King Evander. These people are enemies of the Latins, and will gladly join forces with you. Row upstream till you find them; my current will turn and carry you along."

Aeneas woke, refreshed in mind and body. He ordered two ships to be made ready to row up the river, and wandered to the water's edge to offer a prayer to the god. The grass on the riverbank was particularly green and lush, so Aeneas could not at first see what was making a strange combination of grunts and squeals and rustling in the undergrowth. Sure enough, there lay a fat white sow, stretched out at full length, while over her ample belly clambered thirty hungry, noisy piglets.

"The gods so far keep faith, Ascanius," Aeneas said,

happily showing Iulus the sow and her litter. "But to make quite sure, we will sacrifice these to mighty Juno."

For two days, Aeneas and his picked crews rowed up the Tiber, which had become miraculously smooth and easy. They were in good spirits, and sang as they worked the oars. The weather was fine and warm, the water cool and clear, and a light breeze brought them the fresh, tingling scent of the forest.

The buildings of Pallanteum were clustered about a hill. As the Trojans approached, they could see people gathered outside the small town, and could smell the smoke and incense of a sacrifice. King Evander was presiding over a festival in honour of Hercules, who was worshipped as a local hero in Pallanteum. The ritual banquet was interrupted when the Trojan ships appeared. Everyone leapt up, exclaiming and pointing. The king's son, a youth called Pallas, immediately drew his sword and ran to the bank, calling boldly, "Who are you? Do you come in peace or war?"

Aeneas rose, and held up an olive branch for all to see: "We are Trojans. We visit you in peace. We have come to find King Evander, to make a treaty with him against our common enemy, the Latins."

Pallas sheathed his sword at once. "You are welcome, friends. Come ashore and meet my father the King."

Old King Evander had a frank, benevolent face, and his greeting was hospitable enough, and yet Aeneas stammered nervously as he began his speech. Evander was a Greek, and now the Trojans had to ask favours of him. "Sir, Fate has driven me to seek your help," he began. "I am not sorry, for I have heard of your noble character, and besides, it appears that we are related by blood.

Dardanus, the founder of Troy, was the grandson of mighty Atlas, who holds up the sky. Your ancestor, I am told, was Mercury, the gods' immortal messenger, and Mercury, as you know, is also a grandson of Atlas. Therefore your race and mine have common roots.

"If this formal speech was all I had to say, sir, I could have sent an official embassy. But I have come in person to beg for your aid. The Latins have banded together to drive us out of Italy. If you join forces with us, we may be able to beat them. We are few in number, but no weaklings in war. If you help us, we will not disappoint you."

Aeneas waited anxiously for Evander's reaction. For some time the Greek King had been staring intently at Aeneas' features, and now he exclaimed, "How like your father you are! Don't look so astonished. I remember Anchises well. Long before you were born, before that terrible war, your Trojan King, Priam, used to pay visits to his sister in Greece. Your father always travelled with him, and they made a regular stop at our home in Arcadia. I was a young fellow then, younger than Pallas here, and Anchises was my special hero. He was the tallest and bravest of all the Trojan party. I remember how I used to hang around, hoping he would notice me. One day he did; he shook my hand, and gave me presents before he left: a quiver, a cloak with gold embroidery, and a pair of golden bridles. I still treasure them; my son Pallas uses them now.

"So, son of Anchises, don't speak to me of begging for aid! Here is my hand, and my everlasting friendship. We'll talk business tomorrow; tonight you must join our feast."

While they were eating and drinking, King Evander explained to the Trojans why his people paid honour to

Hercules: "He rid this place of a horrific, fire-breathing ogre, known by the name of Cacus, who used to live in a cave in that mountain there, terrorising the countryside for miles around.

"The story is that Hercules was passing through this area, on the way back from one of his famous Labours, driving a herd of cattle. As soon as the greedy ogre smelled the herd, he crept out of his lair and hauled off four bulls and four cows by their tails, and walled them up in his cave. The poor beasts mooed in terror, and brought Hercules rushing to the cliffside, brandishing his enormous club of knotted wood. But what was he to do? There was no way in. Three times he ran round the mountain, roaring with rage, looking for an opening, but there was none. Finally, he climbed the side of the cliff, leaned against the peak, took a deep breath, and pushed with all his might. There was a tremendous crack, and the top of the mountain, boulders, trees, soil and all, tumbled into the valley below.

"Hercules could now see straight down into the ogre's den, where his cattle were imprisoned, but he could not reach to pull them out. In vain he flung rocks down on Cacus, who retorted by belching out clouds of flame and smoke that turned the mountain into a fiery volcano. Hercules could not bear the creature's insolence; he leapt down into the cave, and after a struggle that shook the earth until the forest shifted and the river overflowed its banks, he strangled the ogre with his bare hands. Then he pushed out the rock that was wedged in the cave's entrance, and set his cattle free.

"Once Cacus was dead, the whole region flourished.

And that is why we pay tribute to Hercules, Jupiter's mighty son."

The Trojans listened to the legend with great admiration, and Aeneas resolved to make the worship of Hercules a tradition in his own kingdom.

As King Evander escorted Aeneas to the town after the feast, he pointed out various landmarks, and told his guest something of the history of the area: "They say the god Saturn ruled here once and that in his time the people led such peaceful, pure and honest lives that the period was called the Golden Age. But gradually men grew wicked and greedy, and life became harsh. You see how we live today, Aeneas, beset by wars and a constant struggle for survival."

A strange feeling of awe had possessed Aeneas: "What is that hill there, Evander, with a thick wood on the very top? It has a look of majesty, I think. Does it have a name?"

"You are not the first to sense its character, Aeneas. I have heard it called the hill of Jupiter; some people claim that on a dark and stormy day you can see the god poised on the crest, shaking his thunderbolts."

Aeneas could not know that he was looking at the site of the Capitol, one day to be the citadel of Rome and the centre of an empire. He only felt, long after they had entered King Evander's simple house, a strong desire to visit that hill again. But it was late, and there was much to do.

That night the goddess Venus crept softly to the sleeping form of her husband, Vulcan, and kissed him tenderly. It was not something she often did: Vulcan, the fire-god who, with incredible skill, fashioned jewellery and weapons for the other gods and goddesses, was ugly, lame and deformed. Venus had been forced to marry him against her will. Vulcan loved her desperately and hopelessly; her endless number of admirers, mortal and divine, kept him in a constant fever of jealousy.

"Darling," Venus was now murmuring in his ear, "will you do just one small favour for me? I have never asked you for anything before, not even when my precious Troy was going up in flames."

"That's half the trouble," Vulcan grumbled. "You don't think I'm any use for anything. If you wanted me to help the Trojans, why didn't you ask? I have been known to produce a weapon or two!"

"How clever of you to guess what I was thinking of!" Venus exclaimed, nestling close to him and rubbing her cheek against his. "My son, Aeneas, is about to fight a terrible battle against overwhelming numbers of Latins. You once supplied a set of armour for the Greek Achilles; will you do as much for my son? Do you promise?"

Vulcan did not think of refusing. Delighted at the chance to please his beautiful wife, he shambled off to his underground smithy, deep in the bowels of volcanic Mount Etna. In that immense workshop the labourers were Cyclopes, the enormous one-eyed giants, who toiled unceasingly to fulfil the demands of the gods. Night and day the cavern was filled with hammering, bubbling, hissing, and clanking as metals were melted and twisted and forced into a thousand shapes.

Vulcan paused in the high doorway, and nodded in approval at the scene of industry. At one end of the workshop three giants were assembling Jupiter's thunderbolts; the king of the gods needed a continuous supply. In other areas special orders were being completed

— a war-chariot for Mars, and an elaborate shield for Minerva.

The fire-god struck a massive gong. Except for the bubbling of the cauldrons, all noise ceased. The Cyclopes dropped their hairy, sweating arms and lifted their brutish faces to their master.

"Attention! All hands to an urgent job. A set of armour fit for a hero. The best you can do, a top-class effort! It's a special order from the goddess Venus." The workers smirked, winked grotesquely with their single eyes, and lumbered off to obey.

At first light, Evander and Aeneas, accompanied by Achates and young Pallas, were settling down in serious conference. "I have thought carefully about the best plan of action," Evander began. "I only wish we Arcadians could be more help to you, Aeneas. But as you can see for yourself, our numbers are few and we are hemmed in by the Latins. However, there is a good chance of getting yourself a very strong ally, if you are prepared to move fast."

"Just tell me how," Aeneas responded at once.

"The Etruscans live a short distance from here. They used to be ruled by a tyrant called Mezentius, more like a monster than a man. He openly defied the gods, and his favourite hobby was devising new forms of hideous torture. Then there was a rebellion. Mezentius somehow escaped alive, along with his son Lausus, and took refuge with our mutual friend, the noble Turnus. The Etruscans are still thirsting for revenge, and at this very moment are camped in arms, intending to force Turnus to surrender his guest to justice."

Aeneas looked at Achates, who smiled and nodded.

"They would surely combine forces with us."

"They are bound to, Aeneas. For they have heard an oracle saying that they must find a commander for this war who is not Italian-born. They even approached me, but I am too old for active service. You are the very man they need, Aeneas. You will surely lead a triumphant army against Turnus and the Latins."

Aeneas was already buckling on his sword-belt. "May the gods reward you, Evander. I'll leave at once for the Etruscan camp."

"Wait one moment more. I said I would help you as much as I could. Four hundred Arcadian cavalry, fully equipped, are ready to escort you. And to show you the faith I have in your success, I am sending Pallas along to serve as your squire."

The youth jumped up and hugged his father joyfully. "I can really fight?"

"The day had to come, my son. You could have no better model than Aeneas. Watch him carefully, and do exactly as you are told. I hope you will prove a soldier."

Aeneas and Achates, both seasoned warriors, smiled at the enthusiasm of the young recruit, but the glances they exchanged were serious. The day of battle was very near; no one could tell whose blood would flow before it ended, or whose the victory would be.

The preparations were quickly made. Old King Evander took leave of Pallas. He had intended to send him off with a rousing, patriotic speech, but he forgot the words he had carefully composed, and wept and clung to the youth like any ordinary father, begging the gods to protect his son from harm.

Aeneas selected a small band of Trojans to accompany

him to the Etruscan stronghold, and despatched the rest in
the ships to report to Iulus. In a few hours Aeneas, with
Achates on one side and Pallas on the other, was riding
through the guardposts of the Etruscan camp and admiring
the obvious size and strength of their army. King Tarchon,
a dark, stocky man who rarely smiled, was waiting at the
doorway of his headquarters. He received the Trojans and
their escort briskly, taking their alliance for granted, and
assigned them to lodgings in his camp.

Venus waited till Aeneas was alone, and then appeared
before him, carrying the most magnificent set of armour he
had ever seen. She did not stay to hear his amazement or
his thanks, but soared into the clouds and disappeared.
Gingerly at first, Aeneas picked up the weapons that
glittered at his feet. The helmet had plumes the colour of
flame. He flourished the sword and the spear, testing their
weight and balance. The breastplate was fashioned from
dark bronze, almost blood-coloured; the greaves, fitting his
legs exactly, were gold inlaid with amber.

Last of all, he raised the shield, and gazed at its design in
wonder. The surface was covered with figures and famous
scenes from the future history of Rome, the nation that
would spring from Aeneas' people. He stroked the metal
gently, admiring the skill of the master-craftsman, and
puzzling over the variety of scenes and actions. He was
fascinated by the vigour and energy that shone from each
figure.

There lay a she-wolf, fondling two baby boys, the twins
Romulus and Remus; next to it a crowd of Sabine women
struggled to escape from the Roman youths carrying them
off; the hero Horatius, single-handed, guarded the bridge
across the Tiber; on the Capitol Hill, a goose flapped its

wings in alarm as a line of Gauls, knives between their teeth, scaled the cliff to attack Rome's citadel. There were parades of priests and ladies, and scenes of criminals in torment. A sea-battle was in full swing, on a sea of silver and gold. One fleet of bronze ships was commanded by the gleaming figure of Caesar Augustus, the other by Mark Antony and Cleopatra, queen of Egypt.

The final scene showed a long procession of conquered nations, from every corner of the earth. Surrounded by altars and offerings, the Emperor Augustus sat calmly surveying them from a shining throne, and accepted their tribute.

Aeneas laughed in delight. He could not understand these scenes, set in the distant future, but he swung the shield onto his left arm. Its size and weight were exactly right.

IX   Turnus Attacks the Trojan Camp

IRIS glided to earth on her rainbow wings, and dropped neatly beside Turnus. "Why not attack the Trojans now?" she whispered. "Aeneas is far away. One quick move, and their camp is yours!"

Juno, watching from above, smiled as her message was delivered. She knew Turnus would not delay.

The Trojan camp was protected by a wooden stockade set on top of a ramp of firmly-packed earth. A watch-tower stood at each corner. It was from one of these that a sentry noticed a thin, but spreading, smudge on the horizon. To his trained eyes it had only one possible meaning.

"Sound the alarm!" ordered Mnestheus, the camp commander, as soon as he heard the sentry's report.

Many of the Trojans were outside the defences, some hunting, some drawing water from the river, others working on the ships. The repeated blare of trumpets brought them to the gates at a run. Aeneas had left very clear orders. If the enemy attacked, no one was to venture out to fight in the open. So the gates were barricaded, the guard-posts and catwalks were manned, and the Trojans waited.

The enemy drew closer. Turnus, with his triple-plumed gold helmet, could easily be distinguished from the rest, especially when he suddenly galloped ahead of the line. He threw back his head to roar a challenge, so that the menacing helmet-plumes jerked and nodded, and hurled a spear towards the camp. This was the official declaration of war. His troops responded in chorus with a oath, and a well-drilled flourish of glittering weapons. The Trojans remained still.

The Latin ranks halted, just out of bowshot, but Turnus advanced alone, heedless of danger. A spear-length from the gate he reined his horse so sharply that it reared in protest. He shouted above its frantic neighing: "Come out and fight, you cowards!" There was no response from the defenders.

Turnus wheeled and skirted the ramp, eyeing the sturdy barrier. Frustrated, he wheeled again, and set off at full tilt in the opposite direction. There was no way into the camp. He stopped once more. Latins and Trojans watched the tossing plumes and the powerful arms that held the plunging horse in check.

Then, "Burn their ships!" Turnus roared and galloped away to the river-mouth. The Trojan fleet lay moored to the bank where the Tiber met the sea. Small watch-fires flickered by the water's edge, and here and there were scattered piles of rope, planking, tar and iron rivets.

Turnus leaned down and caught hold of a stout piece of wood. Behind him he heard the shouts of some of his Rutulian troops. With another yell of "Burn the ships!" he passed the stake through a bucket of tar and made for the nearest fire. The others were quick to follow his example. Triumphantly waving their flaming fire-brands, they crowded the bank, waiting for the word of command.

And there and then, as they drew back their arms to

throw, a blinding light flashed from the sky, a cloud appeared from nowhere, and a deafening crash, like the sound of giant cymbals, shattered the very air. From the centre of the cloud rang a female voice: "How dare you, Turnus? These ships are formed from the sacred pines of Mount Ida. I, the Great Mother, gave a loan of my living trees, until such time as the Trojans should reach their promised land. The time has come. Go, my lovely children, swim fast and free!"

The mooring-ropes snapped. The ships drifted a few yards, then dived prow-first, into the current. At the edge of the sea they surfaced, shooting up like dolphins, but they were not dolphins. Each ship was now a beautiful maiden, a nymph of the sea. They dived again in unison, and vanished.

Turnus was at a loss, but only for a moment. "You see!" he cried to his trembling, pale-faced warriors. "Even their ships are terrified of us!" One man giggled nervously, as if expecting a vengeful blow from the sky. But the strange cloud was gone, and the other soldiers joined in a roar of laughter that was, perhaps, a little too hearty.

"Well, men," Turnus continued, "we can say that was an omen. But make no mistake, that omen was on our side. The gods have cut off the Trojans' only way of escape and presented them to us, trapped in their camp. You have all heard the story of Troy. A mighty city that was — and what happened to it? Burned to the ground. Look at this camp — a pile of dirt with a fence on top! Do we need a Wooden Horse to break in?"

The ripple of answering laughter was confident now. "We'll let them stew until tomorrow. Then we'll fire the camp and smoke the cowards out!"

The main body of the Latin army were soon pitching tents on the plain, while fourteen hand-picked Rutulian officers, each with a hundred men, stood guard around the Trojan camp. They lit a ring of watch-fires, and prepared to wait through the night.

Inside the camp there was furious activity, as the Trojans tried to make the most of the few hours they had. Beams, planks and even furniture were brought to strengthen the walls; extra men were assigned to the weakest points, and the crack troops were stationed at the gates.

At one gate stood Nisus and Euryalus, the two comrades who had run in the foot-race in Sicily. Nisus, always hot-tempered, found the tense hours of darkness more than he could bear. "This is ridiculous," he stormed. "Look at them, just waiting till it's convenient to come in and finish us off. There's not a doubt in their minds — I saw them issuing wine to the guards. They don't even think we are worth staying sober for."

"They're singing," commented Euryalus, peering at the flickering fires.

"Soon they'll be out cold. What a chance for us! But no: we must just wait meekly till they wake up, ready to kill us!"

"We can't possibly attack them," Euryalus, always more realistic, reminded him. "There are thousands of them out there. Even if we killed the pickets, which is risky enough in the dark, the whole of the army would come down on us. If they take the camp, they've got us. We have nowhere to hide. We have to wait for Aeneas, and hope he comes soon, with reinforcements."

"We can hope," Nisus retorted, "but how is Aeneas to know what's going on here? He's probably feasting and swapping stories with the Arcadians, forgetting about us."

"Aeneas never forgets about us," Euryalus said. "Still, I wish he would hurry back."

"That's it!" Nisus exclaimed. "Aeneas has to be told. Listen, it's quiet out there. I bet they're all asleep. I'm going to slip through their lines and run to Pallanteum to find Aeneas."

"Nisus!" his friend exlaimed, "Not by yourself!"

"It's safer alone. One man could sneak through the lines and be away before they heard."

"So could two. It's a risk, and I doubt if our commanders will approve, but if you go, then so do I."

"Euryalus, don't be a fool! There's no point in both of us risking our lives. Besides, there's your mother — the only old lady who refused to stay in Sicily — did she come all this way just to lose her son?"

"She could lose him any time, and she knows it," Euryalus replied calmly. "Let's get someone to relieve us, and pay a call on the high command."

They found the senior officers in conference, among them Iulus, whose boyish features had hardened a good deal since the time of that unfortunate hunt. Nisus saluted, and without waiting for permission to speak, launched into his proposal: ". . . and we have often been hunting up the course of the river, and know the way to Pallanteum well, even in the dark," he concluded.

The first to respond was old Aletes. "May the gods bless you both! The spirit of old Troy is strong in men like you. If you can bring this off, I'll say you deserve the highest rewards heaven and earth can supply!"

Iulus agreed: "Yes! If you can get through to my father, and bring him back in time to save us, I promise you enough gold to make you rich for the rest of your lives.

And if we beat Turnus, I'll see that you, Nisus, get his horse, his helmet and his shield to keep for yourself. And you, Euryalus — you're only a bit older than me — you will be my best friend and my comrade-in-arms!"

Euryalus, greatly moved, could only stammer, "Just one favour, sir. My mother — you know her, she's the only old lady in the camp — will you look after her? I don't want to tell her I'm going. She would make a fuss, sir. But if I knew she was going to be all right . . ."

"Don't worry," Iulus broke in. "I'll treat her like my own mother, I swear it. Now you must take my sword for luck."

They slipped out of the gate facing the river, and made for the nearest watch-fire, now only a peaceful glow in the darkness. They could hear the heavy breathing of drunken sleepers, and smelt the sweat of their huddled bodies. Nisus drew his sword, and whispered, "This is it. We have to cut our way through." Euryalus saw him dimly by the sinking firelight, stooping over a snoring figure and thrusting with his right arm. The figure gave a grunt and dropped back. Nisus moved ahead, and another heavy form slumped to the ground. Euryalus gritted his teeth, stepped over an outstretched leg, and collided with a crouching soldier who was wide awake. He struck, and the Rutulian dropped before he could utter his cry of alarm.

The next few moments were grim. Finally, Nisus gasped, "We're through. Quick, it's nearly light! We can run for it now." Euryalus snatched up a plumed helmet belonging to the chieftain Messapus, and bolted after his friend, putting on the trophy as he ran.

Suddenly they heard galloping hooves and a shout of command. They froze, aware that they were still in the

open. "Despatch-riders for Turnus," muttered Nisus. "They'll mow us down. Count to three, and then run for the cover in those trees."

"Halt! Who goes there?" The leader had seen the gleam of Euryalus' prize helmet. "After them!"

The Trojans darted into the safety of the wood. Nisus, who knew the path well, ran at full speed through the narrow clearing. Euryalus, still fumbling with the strap of his new helmet, fell behind, tripped over some brambles, lost the path, and crashed in confusion through the thick undergrowth, announcing his presence clearly.

Running furiously, Nisus reached the outskirts of the wood. He leaned on his spears and swayed forward, gulping hungrily for air. Then he realized that he was alone. Reeling with exhaustion and shock, he turned to stumble back. A pale light had begun to filter through the leaves. The wood that had been a dark and comforting haven was now full of treacherous, ghostly shadows.

He dared not call out, not even in a whisper. But all at once the wood filled with noise: shouts of alarm, hooves trampling the bushes, and the unmistakable clash of metal on metal. Nisus' quick footsteps were drowned by the din.

He had guessed, but now he saw. Nine or ten horsemen, leaping from their mounts, had closed with Euryalus, who, backed against a tree, was defending himself with sword and shield. Nisus flung a spear at the nearest enemy, a broad-shouldered fellow who was raising his sword to strike. The spear caught him in the back; he lurched forward and fell. At once his companions spun round, and a second spear struck one of them full in the face, killing him instantly.

"We'll soon fix your friend!" a third soldier snarled, and

plunged his blade through the breastplate of Euryalus. Nisus screamed a warning − too late − and hurled himself on his friend's killer. There was a short, fierce duel; the Rutulian, at last, sank to his knees, dying. But by now Nisus was utterly spent; wounded many times, he collapsed on to his friend's body, and lay still.

In the light of early morning, Turnus reviewed a line of bodies, laid out in a gruesome parade of death. No fewer than fourteen soldiers had been killed outside the camp, and, in addition, three despatch-riders. Turnus looked at the two young Trojans who lay side by side, Euryalus still wearing the helmet he had been so proud to capture. "Give Messapus back his helmet," he snapped, "and tell him to take better care of it in future. As for these two, we'll fix their heads on spears, and march them round the Trojan camp to discourage any other heroics."

No one told the mother of Euryalus, but she, noticing that everyone seemed to be out, left her quarters and joined the crowd lining the walls. "What's all that shouting?" she asked a soldier. "I can't quite see. Are they trying to frighten us with their noisy parade?"

The soldier looked at her, and, without answering, moved aside and pointed. The old lady peered intently at the column of Latins, chanting as they paraded their grisly trophies. Then she let out a wail so piercing that even the marching troops broke off their chant and stared up at the wall.

Her cry rang out again and again. She called her son's name, she cursed the war, the Fates and the enemy, and pleaded with the gods to strike her dead. The Trojan officers, headed by Iulus, rushed to console her, but she pushed them aside and went on screaming. Ilioneus, worried that her grief might spread panic, gave brisk orders, and two burly soldiers picked up the old woman and carried her away from the crowd.

From the main body of the Latin army the war-trumpets sounded; an answering blare came from the ranks of Turnus' hand-picked troops. The Trojans on the walls tested their bows, checked their stockpiles of heavy boulders, and braced themselves for the onslaught.

A troop of Latins charged at the gates in a tight square, each man holding his shield above his head, like a vast tortoise-shell. The defenders heaved down rock after rock, but most of these bounced off the roof of shields, until finally a huge boulder shattered the "tortoise", rolling the men in all directions.

The camp was under attack from every side. Mezentius, the ex-tyrant of the Etruscans, hurled firebrands at the wooden stockade, and peppered the Trojans with deadly slingshots. Others rushed up with ladders and attempted to climb over the wall to fight on the catwalks. A watch-tower caught alight and collapsed, crushing its defenders to death. The air was thick with missiles and the groans of the wounded.

Amid all the commotion, Turnus' brother-in-law, a big warrior by the name of Numanus, was strutting about importantly and bawling insults at the Trojans: "Cowards! Wife-stealers! Make way for the second Fall of Troy!"

Iulus had been glaring at this braggart for some time. Officially, the prince was too young to fight, and was supposed to be hiding with the women and children. In fact, he was in the front-line of defenders, firing rapidly with his hunting-bow. The loud voice and insolent gait of Numanus were too much for him. He notched a fresh arrow, paused to whisper a vow to Jupiter, and drew the bowstring back to his ear. With a twang that rumbled like thunder from heaven, the arrow sped from his bow and passed clean through the braggart's grinning face.

"A present from Troy!" Iulus shouted. The Trojans cheered, and fought on with renewed determination. Although Iulus was eager to prove himself further, the senior officers, knowing his life to be most precious, urged him to retire to safety: "The god of archers, Apollo himself, would not wish you to risk your life. Without you, the future of our race is lost."

The wooden wall and the ramp outside it were now swarming with Trojans and Latins, grappling hand-to-hand. Men as well as missiles were flying from the walls, their yells breaking through the whine of the arrows and rattle of slingshots. The blare of trumpets never ceased. The battle throbbed with its own horrid pulse — the steady clash of metal and the low-pitched, grumbling war-drum. Still the defences held.

At one of the gates two Trojan brothers, Pandarus and Bitias, had beaten off a heavy attack. They were thrilled with the taste of victory. "Give our regards to Turnus!" Pandarus jeered after retreating troops. "Tell him to send men next time!"

Bitias would not be outdone. "Here, not so fast!" he called. "Why such a rush to get away? Look, we'll give you an easy chance — try again, girls!" With a peal of confident laughter, he drew the bar and swung back the gate.

At this a small band of Latins turned and rushed for the opening. The two brothers, still laughing, picked them off with their spears, and blocked the entrance with their bodies. Other Latins, however, took up the cry, "The gate! The gate!" and surged forward in crowds.

The call reached Turnus. He made for the gate at once, brandishing his deadly pair of spears. His temper rose high when he saw the impudent brothers, poised on top of the gateposts, inviting attack. It took only a moment to aim. The mighty weapon caught Bitias in the chest; he reeled, and crashed to the ground in a heap of jangling armour.

The fall of Bitias gave the enemy courage. As one they stormed the gate, Turnus in the lead, while Trojan soldiers dropped into their midst and joined the turmoil of writhing, straining bodies. Pandarus, now regretting his rashness, pushed sharply at the gate and banged it shut, leaving a number of Trojans outside with the enemy, and Turnus, the Latin hero, alone inside the camp.

Pandarus stood facing his brother's killer. "You've made a mistake, Turnus," he spat, "This is not Queen Amata's guest-room. It's the Trojan camp." He flung his spear; it missed, and stuck fast in the gate.

"What a shame!" mocked Turnus, and lifting his sword high in both hands, brought it down on the young man's head.

That was only the beginning. Turnus, crazy for Trojan blood, did not think of opening the gate and letting his soldiers in. He hacked left and right, strewing the ground with mangled bodies and driving a shock of fear through the Trojan ranks. Man after man he killed, while the defenders scattered in panic at his advance.

Mnestheus hurried to the scene. "What's the matter with you all?" he cried above the tumult. "There's only one man here, and he's mortal. Aeneas would be ashamed to see you now!"

Then the Trojans closed in, and Turnus was forced to give ground. Inch by inch, he backed closer to the wall, parrying with his huge shield the blows that rained down on him. Twice he lunged forward and slashed with his deadly sword. But Mnestheus was in the lead now, fighting with cold determination. Turnus' head was ringing with the blow that had cracked his gaudy helmet; his limbs were drenched in sweat, and his breath was failing. With a final effort he swung up to a platform overlooking the Tiber, and, with a roar of defiance, threw himself fully-armed into the water below.

The current was kind; it bathed his wounds, and restored him, still unconquered, to his anxious troops.

X   Aeneas Joins the Battle

"I HAVE summoned you all," Jupiter announced, "to settle this abominable strife that is tearing apart the peaceful land of Latium." In the great hall of Olympus, walled with cloud and roofed with a thousand stars, the immortal gods sat in council.

"This is not the time decreed for war," rumbled the king of the gods. "That time will come, when the fierce troops of Carthage will ravage Italy and threaten the walls of mighty Rome. But not yet, not now! Trojans and Latins have no real cause to quarrel. This war must cease!"

Ceres, the corn-goddess, agreed with an approving, motherly smile: "My fields are looking dreadfully neglected. I'm afraid there won't be much of a harvest in Latium, but by next year . . ."

"Nonsense!" Mars broke in. "Toughen them up a bit! What use is a race of weaklings?"

"Silence!" Jupiter roared above the outbreak of comment. "We are not here for a general debate. I have said . . ."

"Father, listen to me." Venus clasped her hands imploringly and gazed at him as only she could do. "Father, look at the plight of the Trojans. They are prisoners in their own camp, valiantly defending their lives, while Turnus flaunts himself on the battlefield like a hero, knowing full well that Aeneas is away. But is this the will of Fate – that Troy should perish a second time? Have you forgotten how the ships were nearly burnt in Sicily? You had to save them yourself, father. What about the storm and the shipwreck at Carthage? Who brought that about?"

"Someone with no business to be meddling in my kingdom," growled Neptune. Juno remained silent.

"We all know who it was," Venus continued. "And now, since heaven and earth can't help her any more, she has gone so far as to call on the hellish fiend Allecto to stir up strife in Latium. This is too much! What use was the escape from Troy and the years of suffering and hope if, after all, the Trojans are butchered by Turnus? My little grandson, Ascanius – is there no future for him? Father, I appeal to you, can the sacred decrees of Fate be blotted out at the whim of one spiteful goddess?"

"Hypocrite!" Juno had risen now. "Who caused the Fall of Troy? Who sent the Trojan Paris to elope with Helen of Sparta? You! You should have thought of your precious Trojans a little sooner. And now that Aeneas has invaded a foreign land – don't you quote Fate at me! – aren't the owners entitled to defend it? Is Turnus to stand meekly by while he is cheated of his rightful bride? When you use your powers to save Aeneas, that's fine! But if I lift a finger to help Turnus, whose mother is divine and whose family tree is not to be sneered at – if I help him, then I am wicked and spiteful!"

"Order!" Jupiter's deep voice stilled the general clamour. "All of you, hear my pronouncement. Since it has come to pass, for whatever reason, that Trojans and Latins are waging war in Italy, I, the king of gods and men, declare myself impartial. Let each nation do its best; I view them both alike, and leave the result to Fate."

Meanwhile, the Trojans were finding it harder and harder to defend their camp. Their numbers were small; when a man died on the wall, there was none to take his place. The enemy, in contrast, brought up fresh troops in hundreds, wave after wave. The camp was ringed with fire. Most of the watch-towers had crumbled. The young son of Aeneas was back at the wall, firing arrows thick and fast at the enemy, but now no one urged him away. Every pair of hands was needed. No one said it, but they were all praying that Aeneas would return before it was too late.

In fact, Aeneas was not far away. Tarchon, the Etruscan leader, had proved prompt and efficient. It was quickest, he had said, to transport the army by sea, except for the main force of Arcadian cavalry who were despatched overland. And so, at the very hour of night when Nisus was proposing his ill-fated plan, they had embarked, thirty vessels and a good five thousand men. Etruscans and allies alike, all had accepted Aeneas as their commander.

The night was still. In a graceful line, the fleet moved southwards along the coast. The leading ship, marked by its lion-shaped prow, contained the small Trojan force, a number of Arcadian horsemen, and Aeneas himself, who stood at the helm with young Pallas, explaining to him how to steer by the stars. The night wore on, until at last only Aeneas and the oarsmen were still awake.

The Trojan hero was glad to steer the ship, for he was too worried to sleep. The steady beat of the oars and the ripple of the sea were beginning to calm his nerves, when suddenly, all around the ship, he heard leaps and splashes and voices calling his name.

He spun round in alarm, to see a shapely maiden swinging from the stern-rail, her wet body shimmering in the moonlight. "Don't be startled, Aeneas," she said. "We're your friends, my sisters and I. We were once your ships, which you built from Mount Ida's sacred pinetrees. Turnus tried to burn us at our moorings, but the Great Mother came to our rescue. She turned us into sea-nymphs and we swam away. Now we have urgent news for you. Your son is in grave danger. Turnus has besieged the Trojan camp, knowing you are not there. He plans to attack at dawn with an enormous army. You must hurry, Aeneas. Your men cannot hold out for long. We will help you make good speed; you will reach the Tiber at daybreak. But be ready to fight for your life!" She dropped back into the waves with a splash. Aeneas gripped the tiller hard, and the ship shot forward like an arrow, propelled by superhuman force.

When the first rays of dawn touched the waves, Aeneas roused his men from sleep and ordered them to arm themselves. As they neared the Tiber's mouth, the din of battle reached them clearly over the water.

Aeneas, a dazzling figure in the armour of Vulcan, stood ready on the deck. As soon as he sighted the Trojan camp, he raised his splendid shield, and flashed it in the sunlight. From the distant camp came an answering cheer.

Turnus, fresh from his exploits within the Trojan defences, looked round and saw the line of ships, their decks glittering with weapons. "Well, men, here's the chance we've been waiting for," he called to his troops. "You have all been saying you wanted a chance to fight in the open, instead of dodging round this chicken-coop. Let's meet them on the beach. Remember, it's our land they're invading, our wives and children they'll kidnap and murder, if we let them. Every man to his post!"

Aeneas waited till the keels scraped the sand, then ordered the gangways to be lowered. From thirty ships came a rattle of heavy chains and a creaking of hinges. "All ashore!" was the next command, and the waist-deep water became a threshing turmoil of men and armour. Not all made a graceful landing: Tarchon's ship struck a hidden reef, broke its keel and, plummeting violently, threw its crew overboard in confusion.

From the ranks of waiting Latins the war-trumpets brayed defiantly. Turnus held his troops in check, letting the enemy stagger awkwardly through the shallows and up the muddy sand, weighed down with sword, shield, spears and body-armour.

Aeneas led the battle-charge, with faithful Achates close by his side. Not since the last days of Troy had they engaged in serious fighting, but their skills were practised and their weapons keen. Beginning with sword and shield, Aeneas cut a deadly path through the enemy ranks. Spears were hurled at him in dozens, but they bounced harmlessly away from his shining armour. Two huge men lunged at him with clubs; he struck them both to the ground. Sheathing his sword, he took from Achates a bundle of spears. His aim was true: each spear found a tender mark, piercing the thickest breastplates of bronze and leather.

Meantime, young Pallas, with a small escort of mounted Arcadians, had swum his horse to land. He intended to skirt the throng of battling footsoldiers, and make contact with the main company of Arcadian cavalry which had made the journey overland. But the path up from the beach was steep and rough, and they had to dismount, and lead the horses. No sooner had they reached level ground than they found themselves faced with a large and menacing enemy band. There was no time to mount.

"Shall we charge, sir?" With a thrill of fear Pallas realized that the grey-haired soldier was addressing him. Though completely untried in battle, he was now in command. He ran his tongue over his lips, knotted his trembling fingers round his spear-shaft and called, "Men of Pallanteum, our only hope is attack! Follow me!"

He rushed at the enemy. A man blocked his way, grinning, with a huge boulder aimed at his head. Pallas caught him in the ribs with his spear, and as he fell, wrenched the weapon free. The man's breath gurgled from him as he died. His comrade dashed at Pallas with sword and shield; the young man ducked, and drove his blade upwards deep into the fellow's lungs.

After this, there was no hanging back. Pallas struck and parried blow after blow. His Arcadian troops, though not used to fighting on foot, took their courage from him, and pressed bravely through the jostling ranks.

Cleaving a path through Etruscans and Arcadians came Lausus, son of the ex-tyrant, Mezentius. Unlike his vicious father, Lausus was a frank-faced, popular youth. His bravery and leadership in battle were already well proven, and he was a useful captain in Turnus' army. Pallas drew level with him, and the two young men circled each other, watching for a chance to strike. They were about equal in age and build, and might have been friends if their fates had been different.

The soldiers on both sides fell back a little, seeing their young leaders braced for a duel. Resting their spears, like a crowd at a sporting-match, they began to urge on their champions by name.

Suddenly there was a commanding shout, "Leave Pallas to me!" and speeding through the throng in a resplendent chariot came Turnus. He jumped to the ground and addressed his enemy: "Get ready to die, my boy. I only wish I had your father Evander here to see."

Pallas looked up at the massive shoulders and the flamboyant crest that towered above him, and answered, "I wish he was here, too. Because then he could see me kill you, Turnus, or else die like a glorious warrior myself."

The spectators gasped as Pallas gripped his spear and stepped to meet his fate, crying on Hercules, his patron, to protect him. He balanced the shaft, and threw. The spear flew fast, clipped the edge of Turnus' shield, and grazed his shoulder. Since he had no second spear, Pallas drew his sword and crouched behind his shield as Turnus took aim.

The spear that Turnus threw was made of heavy oak, with a head of steel. With the force of a mighty arm to drive it, it whistled through the air and pierced right through shield and breastplate into the flesh of Pallas. He reeled, staring dumbly at the spear-head that pinned his shield to his chest; then jerked his left arm and tore the weapon out. The blood came in a gush, and he fell forward.

Turnus rolled Pallas' body face up with his foot. "Tell King Evander," he said to the Arcadians, "that this is his reward for making friends with Aeneas." He bent over the corpse, unfastened Pallas' gold-embossed sword-belt, and slinging it over his shoulder, he stepped into his chariot and drove off.

A runner brought the news to Aeneas: Pallas was dead.

The Trojan leader stopped in the midst of the raging battle, and a terrible look came over his face. He remembered Pallas scampering down to the river bank to meet his ships, and King Evander's ready hospitality. He felt again the clasp of the old man's hand and heard his quavering voice and his tears as he entrusted his only son to the Trojans.

Aeneas had been fighting like a soldier, determined and brave, but now he fought like a madman. "Take these alive!" he roared at Achates, as a terrified group retreated before his slashing sword. "I'll sacrifice them to Pallas later!" A Latin called Magus, ducking his spearthrust, fell at his feet and sobbed for mercy, promising as ransom everything he owned. Aeneas looked down at him, and imagined young Pallas kneeling before the mocking figure of Turnus; he grabbed Magus by his helmet-strap and slit his throat.

A chariot with two drivers crashed through the fray and bore down on Aeneas. With a bloodcurdling war-cry he ran straight at the horses. One of the drivers felt the point of his spear; the other he dragged to the ground and beheaded. The rearing horses threw up dust in clouds.

On high Olympus, Jupiter, with frowning brow, was observing the battle. He noted that the Trojan camp was no longer besieged, that Turnus was rallying all his forces to resist the havoc spread by Aeneas' onslaught. The king of the gods addressed his wife Juno, "You must not blame Venus. You can see for yourself the terrible damage Aeneas has wrought single-handed. The Trojans themselves have shown fierce courage, and the credit for victory must be their own."

"My lord," Juno answered, with unusual meekness, "you

needn't tell me — I can see it all too well. Please, dear husband, grant me one favour. I know I can't save Turnus for ever, but let me keep him from harm for just a little while. He is a good man; he has often paid homage to you. A breathing-space, my lord, please!"

"Now, Juno," said Jupiter sternly, "you must understand, once and for all, that you cannot alter the result of this war. If all you have in mind is a short respite for Turnus, well and good; but if you have any further designs, you may as well give them up now."

Juno did not stay for further discussion. She slipped down to Latium, wrapped in cloud, and landed invisible among the fighters. Then, seizing handfuls of air and mist, she deftly fashioned a likeness of Aeneas with his exact dress and features. She breathed a spell, and the phantom moved and spoke according to her will, but in Aeneas' manner and voice. It strode up to Turnus, and shouted a challenge.

Turnus reacted immediately, hurling his spear. Although his aim was perfect, his target seemed unhurt. It turned away, and began to run. "Stand and fight, you coward!" Turnus roared, and raced in pursuit.

Through the thick of the battle scurried the phantom-Aeneas, till it reached the shore where the ships were beached. With a noiseless leap it boarded the nearest, and vanished among the rigging and sails. Close on its heels came Turnus. "You won't escape now!" he jeered, kicking obstacles aside and slashing at ropes. "What's the matter? Have you decided to give up your claims to my land? I'll give you a plot of land, free — just your size!"

Juno, hovering over the beach, gave the stern of the ship a mighty push. Exclaiming in alarm, Turnus ran to the rail, but already the water below was deep. All around the air was still; yet the sails were full, and the ship streaked over the water like a bird in flight.

Three times Turnus tried to dive overboard, but each time Juno held him back. In tears of rage, he cried to the gods: "You have destroyed my name and honour! How can I ever face my people again, after deserting them in a battle? Send me a quick death now, away from their sight!" The ship sped on regardless, till it reached the coastal town where his elderly father lived, and there it came to rest.

The Latins and their allies were bewildered by the disappearance of Turnus, but they were not long without a leader. Mezentius was quick to assume command. With his son Lausus close behind, he began a riot of slaughter more savage than any seen so far.

The Etruscans, now part of Aeneas' army, had by no means forgotten the hatred for Mezentius that had prompted them to join with the Trojans. Every one of them had mourned the death of a father, a brother, or a son who had suffered horribly at the tyrant's hands. Now they closed in on Mezentius, howling like beasts for his blood.

Mezentius stood quite still before the cursing mob, and his eyes taunted them over the rim of his shield. He did not appear to notice the missiles that rained down on his head and shoulders. Then, with a hideous laugh, he began to kill, picking out individuals by name and dealing out a brutal death to each. One had his head smashed with a boulder; another was hamstrung and left huddled over legs that could not longer stand. No one dared to come within reach of that flashing sword, and when Mezentius began to step forward, the Etruscans backed away.

Aeneas, still hot for revenge on Turnus, emerged from the tumult of the battle to see Mezentius driving before him a pack of terrified soldiers, hypnotized by his swinging blade and mocking laughter. At the same moment, Mezentius caught sight of Aeneas. "Watch this!" he called to his son Lausus. "See that fine suit of armour Aeneas is wearing — I'll present it to you. I swear by my favourite god, which is my own right arm!"

He cast his spear at Aeneas, but the dazzling shield knocked it aside. Now Aeneas took a pace forward, searching his enemy for an unprotected target. There was none: Mezentius was covered from head to foot, and held an enormous shield. Aeneas drew a deep breath, and threw with all his strength. His spear struck the centre of Mezentius' shield, cut through the layers of bronze and fabric and the triple leather lining, and pierced him low in the belly. The Etruscans cheered to see the tyrant wounded, and roared in excitement as Aeneas drew his sword and rushed at their hated enemy.

That would have been the end of Mezentius, but for the courage of his son. Lausus dashed in, intercepted the fatal blow, and covered his father with his own shield. Together they faced Aeneas, Lausus yelling defiance and battering the Trojan leader with a shower of stones.

"Get out of the way, boy!" Aeneas shouted. "You're no match for me!" Lausus shrieked an insult. But a moment later, he was writhing on the ground, his tunic soaked in blood, his cheeks drained of colour.

Aeneas looked at the gasping lad, and imagined Iulus in such a state. His fury turned to sympathy. "Poor boy," he said softly, stroking the dying youth's hand. "You fought like a man. Keep your armour and weapons. Your friends will be able to boast that you died by the sword of Aeneas."

A few yards away, Mezentius was recovering breath. His bodyguard stood by him, bathing his face with water and staunching his wound, while the tyrant cried for news of his son. When he was told, he pulled himself upright despite his searing pain, and called for his horse. "Lift me up to the saddle," he ordered, "and give me my spears. Lausus died for my crimes. He never deserved exile. The Etruscans loved him — he could have stayed at home. But he chose to share my fate."

Two soldiers lifted him into the saddle and handed him his spears. He patted the horse gently, murmuring its name. It whinnied at the familiar voice, and galloped straight into battle.

"Aeneas!" Mezentius bellowed. "Aeneas!" His third call brought the Trojan hero out of the crowd. "Did you think I would let my child die in my place? Take these on his behalf!"

He wheeled at a dizzy pace around Aeneas as he spoke, and threw spear after spear till all were gone. Aeneas spun and dodged, until the ground at his feet and the surface of his shield were bristling with shafts. Then he raised his own spear, sprang high off the ground, and stabbed Mezentius' horse in the forehead. The animal gave a pitiful scream and reared, unseating its master. Then it crashed to the ground on top of Mezentius and lay still.

As Aeneas drew his sword, the Etruscan tyrant gasped, "Don't waste time. Just one favour: protect my body from the Etruscans, and bury me with Lausus. Now strike!"

The sword severed his throat.

XI Turnus is Challenged

"TROJANS, Arcadians, Etruscans, and all faithful allies, we are gathered to dedicate to the god Mars this trophy, the armour and weapons of the hated tyrant, Mezentius. We give thanks for the glorious victory over the forces of Latium which, by the grace of the immortal gods, we won yesterday on this field."

Aeneas paused in his speech, and looked over the soldiers assembled before him. They seemed pleased, but very tired. A number were wounded.

"Today is a day for rejoicing, and celebration. It is also a day of mourning for some of our brave friends, whose names will be honoured for ever among their people. I commend to you especially Pallas, son of our dear friend, King Evander of the Arcadians, who was our first help and support in this new land. It is our sad duty to return to him today the body of his only son, a youth untried in battle, who was not afraid to face the champion Turnus. What a pity the great Turnus had to leave before I could meet him myself! He will not stay out of sight for long. I swear to you, before all the gods, that Pallas will be avenged. Tomorrow we march on the walls of the city. King Latinus will find that he must make good the promises he offered so generously when we arrived."

The men were dismissed. Aeneas smiled at their cheers and returned their salutes. He patted proud young officers on the shoulder, listened to their excited stories, admired the helmets, medallions and shields they had stripped from the enemy, and comforted those who had lost friends and brothers. Within himself he felt drained and dispirited. The battle-fury that had carried him through the previous day had left a bitter taste.

The grass glittered with broken and abandoned weapons. Back and forth from the battle-field the duty-patrols worked, carrying the bodies of their friends to the funeral pyres that smoked along the shore.

"Envoys from the Latins, sir. Request permission to recover their dead from the field." The messengers were anxious, middle-aged men in shabby cloaks, clutching olive branches with both hands. Aeneas granted their request at once.

"Tell King Latinus," he added, "that I have nothing against the people of Latium. If he had kept his word to me, there would be no war at all. But since he has allowed Turnus to take matters into his own hands, tell him that Turnus must answer for his deeds. If Turnus is so set on challenging my right to settle here, let him meet me in single combat. There is no need for thousands of men to risk their lives. The gods will decide between him and me. Go, tell him what I have said."

The envoys bowed, and were making as if to depart, when one of them turned back. He was a skinny, grey-haired man called Drances: "I shall be pleased to report your words to my king, sir. There are many of us who see no cause to fight, and would be happy to see peace restored to Latium. Let Turnus settle his own quarrels, without dragging us all into war."

The other envoys exchanged glances, and nodded. "Then shake hands, friends," Aeneas responded warmly. "Let us agree on a truce to bury our dead. That will give you a chance to persuade your king to call off this war, and honour his promise to us."

"Excuse me, sir," a soldier broke in nervously, "the funeral-party is ready to leave. You said to call you at once."

Pallas lay on a wicker-work bier, wrapped in a robe of royal purple, a gift Queen Dido had made for her cherished Aeneas. In front of the body marched a double file of soldiers, some loaded with trophies, others leading captured horses and pitiful human prisoners. Behind the body of Pallas walked his horse, without saddle or bridle, nuzzling the bier that carried his silent master. After it came an Arcadian officer, with Pallas' helmet and spear; his sword-belt was missing. A column of Trojans, Etruscans and Arcadians, their spears reversed as a sign of mourning, brought up the rear.

Aeneas watched the funeral-procession until it was out of sight. His thoughts were with King Evander.

Rumour had reached Pallanteum, bringing news of a Trojan victory. The people looked forward with joy to the first official report. There were cheers all over the town when the approaching column was sighted. But as the people crowded the hilltops and roofs for a better view, the cheers died away. No one could mistake the slow march and muffled drums for a victory parade. They poured out of the gates — parents, wives, small children — and flocked around the bier, pushing the shining trophies aside.

"Pallas!" The familiar name sounded harsh on the air. The crowd parted to let King Evander through.

His outburst was short and fierce. At last, letting the body drop from his embrace, he said, quite softly, "You promised to be careful, Pallas." Then, remembering himself, he declared in a clear voice: "The Trojans are not to blame. I sent you willingly to join them. I am proud – look at the trophies you won in battle. You fought by the side of Aeneas; what greater glory could a young man want? He is known to be true; I know he will avenge your death."

At that moment Aeneas was not thinking of revenge. Under a sky grey with the sweetish smoke of funeral pyres, he was thinking of peace. Was there any hope in the words of the envoy Drances?

In the city the Laurentes were in turmoil. From every house came sounds of grief. People in the streets were cursing the war and heaping abuse on Turnus for causing it. Others, admiring his spectacular deeds, were arguing loudly that he had a right to claim the hand of the princess Lavinia.

Those in the palace were not any calmer. King Latinus had just received news that the Greek hero, Diomedes, who had fought Aeneas in Troy, now refused to help the Latins against him.

"We visited Diomedes in his Italian settlement," the messengers reported. "He said he has no intention of fighting the Trojan War over again, and risking the anger of the gods. He described Aeneas as a champion warrior, equal to Hector, and noble and true in character, and he advised our people to make peace with the Trojans."

The senior councillors muttered uneasily. King Latinus rose to speak. His breath came in heavy gasps, and his voice had lost its ring of command: "Gentlemen, you have heard the message from Diomedes. This war is pointless. The Trojans are here by the will of the gods. Who are we to oppose them? I propose that we make a fair treaty, grant the Trojans land along the Tiber to build a city, and offer Aeneas a share in the rule of Latium. We will only suffer if we try to resist the Fates' decree."

The councillors buzzed in discussion, most of them favouring the king's proposal. Then suddenly someone shouted outside the hall. There was a scuffle and more shouting, and through the doorway strode Turnus. Eyeing the astonished councillors, he walked around the room slowly. As he reached the throne, he folded his arms, and faced the king.

The council chamber was hushed, but only for a moment. Drances was on his feet: "Your Majesty, I support your words. I have met Aeneas. He is everything a man could wish for in a son-in-law. Let us end this war with a marriage that is blessed by the gods, that will bring peace and added strength to our country. As for you, Turnus – haven't you caused enough death and destruction? How many households are in mourning today in this city, just because Turnus wanted to show off in battle? What gives him a special right to marry the princess? If Turnus has such a desperate desire to win her hand, he should meet Aeneas alone, man to man, and try his courage in single combat. If he refuses, if he insists on sheltering behind an army of thousands, then he is proved unworthy of this royal marriage and must give up his claim."

There was a chorus of support for Drances. Turnus, who had been facing the throne, swung round, strode over to

Drances, seized him by the arm, and hauled him to the centre of the floor: "You're a fine one to talk about single combat, Drances! When was the last time you lifted a spear? Showing off, am I? If you had dared to venture outside these walls during the battle, you would have seen the Tiber red with enemy blood, the insolent tribe of Evander destroyed, and countless Trojans backing away before my charge. You think we're beaten, do you? How many Trojans have you seen inside this city? I had the impression that these walls were still fairly strong, unlike the courage of people like you." He was shaking Drances in his powerful grasp, towering over him head and shoulders. Now he released the councillor so suddenly that he toppled over. "Scared, are you? You needn't worry — I don't waste my strength on enemies like you."

"Turnus," the old king began, "will you listen?"

Turnus faced the throne once more: "I ask your pardon; I could not let such insults pass. To make peace with the Trojans would be a disgrace. Maybe they have gained a temporary advantage; but for every man of ours they killed, we can kill six of theirs. We have mighty allies on our side — look at Camilla with her troop of Volscian cavalry. Have we less courage than a girl? We have a good chance of a glorious victory over the Trojans; but if there is anyone else who thinks I should fight Aeneas in single combat, then just name the day, and I'll be there! I solemnly swear, before you all, to meet Aeneas, alone, in arms, and fight till one of us is killed!"

What King Latinus might have decided was never heard. An alarm-trumpet sounded shrill within the city. A messenger burst into the hall, shouting, "Your Majesty, the Trojans are attacking the city! There are thousands of men sweeping across the plain!"

The king shrank helpless into his seat. Turnus laughed. "Peace, is it? We'd better barricade the gates and man the walls. Will your Majesty give the orders yourself, or trust me to see to them?" And, as the king only hid his face and moaned, Turnus dismissed the panic-stricken councillors and gave orders for the defence of the city. The townsmen were sent to collect stones and pile them in heaps along the battlements. Able-bodied youths dug trenches in front of the gates. A party of noble ladies, led by Queen Amata, climbed the steps of Minerva's temple to offer prayers for victory.

These activities kept the people too busy to panic. Turnus, meanwhile, held a conference with his allied commanders: "My last report said that the cavalry out there is only a band of Etruscan light troops, spread out to look more dangerous than they are. The idea is to keep our attention on them while Aeneas leads the main force round through the hills to attack the city from the rear. That's a trick two can play. You, Camilla, and you, Messapus, will ride out with your troops and engage the Etruscans. They shouldn't give you too much trouble. In the meantime I'll take a picked band of Rutulians out through the rear gate and wait for Aeneas. I know the very place – where the only pass through the hills is narrow and wooded, perfect for an ambush!"

The citizens cheered Camilla as she led her troops through the gates to face the enemy. She was an attractive young woman with steady eyes, dressed in a short hunting-tunic in imitation of her patron goddess, Diana, and armed with battle-axe, spear and bow. Close by her rode a

bodyguard of warrior maidens, armed and equipped like their leader.

The Etruscans were charging at full gallop, howling their war-cry. Camilla waited till they were almost in spear-range, then raised her arm in command. Missiles hummed through the air, and the ground shook with the thunder of hooves.

Since early childhood, Camilla had served the maiden-goddess of hunt and woodland, and Diana loved her dearly in return. Hovering now in the clouds, she was anxiously watching Camilla's progress. She knew the girl's fate, and the knowledge filled her with grief. With a silvery gesture, she summoned her attendant, a fleet-footed nymph called Opis: "Our servant, Camilla, must die in this battle. I cannot prevent her death, but I can avenge it. Follow her closely, Opis, and take the life of the man who kills her."

Twice the Etruscans had charged and retreated before Camilla's volley of spears. Now they made a third attempt at short range. Shields clashed together, and horses and riders were enmeshed in a tangle of limbs and weapons. The dying were trampled by rearing hooves, and the ground grew moist under a steady drizzle of blood.

Every shot of Camilla's was true. Her spears flew from her nimble fingers with deadly speed; her battle-axe smashed a terrible path through enemy helmets.

Tarchon, the Etruscan commander, was roused to fury. "What's the matter with you all?" he roared at his men. "Are you saving your energy for the victory feast? Get in there and fight, instead of shying away from that girl! Watch me, and learn!"

Spurring his horse, he rushed straight at an enemy rider, swept him off his seat in full gallop, and rode on, grappling with the man on his heaving saddle. The Latin seized Tarchon by the throat, desperate to strangle him. Tarchon, in turn, jabbed with the point of his enemy's broken spear, his right arm still clamping the man across his saddle. The horse plunged to and fro with its double burden, till at last Tarchon dropped his victim to the ground, where he slumped in a lifeless heap.

An Etruscan soldier named Arruns, jealous of his general's daring feat, decided to win a share of glory for himself. His goal was Camilla. For a time he circled her at a distance, watching for a chance to cast his spear. But Camilla wheeled and spun like a whirlwind, allowing no weapon to catch her, while she dealt out death on every side. Then she suddenly spotted a man in an unusually splendid outfit; he had once been an eastern priest, and wore embroidered trousers and a yellow cloak fastened with a gaudy brooch; his horse was clad in a coat of bronze scales linked with gold. Camilla's eyes sparkled at the thought of winning such garments. Forgetting all danger, she made straight for her trophy.

Arruns, trailing her closely, saw his chance, and threw. His spear stuck in her breast. She shrieked. Her friends rushed to her side. Arruns was suddenly frightened at his own success. He did not stay to gloat, but melted into the crowd as fast as he could.

Camilla, still conscious, was murmuring to her attendants: "Tell Turnus that he must lead this battle himself. I can do no more to help him." She slipped from her saddle, and died.

The nymph, Opis, on a nearby hillock, saw that Camilla was dead. She fitted an arrow to her golden bow, and shot

Arruns clean through the throat. He never knew who killed him.

Without Camilla, the Latins panicked. They rode in yelling confusion towards the walls of their city, the Etruscans hard on their heels. The gates were barred; they found no way in. On the battlements their own friends were shouting, "Let them in! Open the gates!" but the citizens, seeing only the enemy in pursuit, flung stones and spears on the heads of Etruscans and Latins alike.

News came to Turnus of Camilla's death and the rout of the Latin forces. At once he abandoned his plan of ambush and ordered his troops back to defend the city. Scarcely had he left his position when Aeneas, at the head of the Trojan army, reached the narrow track through the wooded hills. He passed through it easily, and emerged on to the open plain, in time to see Turnus' column making all speed for the city.

The sun was sinking; the Trojans postponed their attack and camped outside the city walls.

XII   The Final Duel

When Turnus entered the city gates, there were no cheers. The people had witnessed Camilla's death, and could see Aeneas' army camped on the plain. Whispers and stares greeted Turnus in the streets, and occasionally a voice would call out: "Call yourself a hero? Then fight your own battles!"

He found King Latinus almost ill with despair, blaming himself again and again for allowing the war to take place. By his side was the queen, now with nothing to say. Lavinia, a pale, modest figure, sat at the end of the room.

"The gods are punishing me," moaned the king. I knew their will, and did not obey it."

"Enough of this!" was the heated response of Turnus. "If everyone thinks I'm to blame for this war, I'm ready and willing to fight for my rights. I'll leave you to arrange the time and place with your friend Aeneas. I'll make him regret the day he set foot on this land. If he wants to marry Lavinia and rule in Latium, he'll have to kill me first!"

King Latinus plucked Turnus' arm in feeble dismay, and tried to look stern: "Turnus, calm down! You are always too hot-tempered. Sit here by me, and listen. Your father is rich and you own acres of good land in Italy. Plenty of pretty girls from good families would be honoured to marry a fine man like you."

"Are you trying to tell me . . . ?"

"Hear me out, boy. You must control your temper. I never should have promised Lavinia to you or to any other Latin prince. If an old man like me can admit a mistake, surely you can do the same. It will be no disgrace to give up your claims. You won't be admitting defeat at enemy hands. Rather, you will be showing yourself the loyal servant of the gods, and what could be more honourable than that? It would be a sheer waste to die on the sword of Aeneas — and die you would, for the gods have decreed that *he* must rule in Latium. Think of your old father at home in Ardea: he would never forgive me for letting you die in a futile attempt to win my daughter."

"Forgive me, sir, but you have too little faith in me. How do you know Aeneas must win? My sword is as sharp as his, my courage sharper. Without his goddess-mother, he is nothing!"

The king sighed and fell back on the couch, burying his face in his shaking hands. Queen Amata's arms were around him at once, and, as she comforted him, she said, "How can you upset us like this, Turnus! If you get yourself killed, what will become of us? I would die rather than become Aeneas' slave!"

Turnus glanced at Lavinia. She blushed and looked away. He bent to kiss the queen on the cheek. "Don't count me dead so soon, madam. You have been a good friend to me; now you must pray for my victory."

A few minutes later a herald was speeding to the Trojan camp with a message for Aeneas: "Turnus agrees to meet the Trojan upstart in single combat at dawn tomorrow.

Let both their armies stand as witnesses. The winner will marry the Princess Lavinia."

Day dawned, brisk and cloudless. The towering walls of the city and the plain below began to fill with spectators. People of all ages crowded the walls. There was a murmur of excitement. From the Trojan camp hardy warriors strolled confidently onto the field. Priests and officials marked out the arena, and set up altars for sacrifices to the gods. On one side a line of Trojan soldiers formed a barrier with their shields and spears; opposite them the Latins did the same.

Inside the city gates Turnus stood by his chariot, a hand on the neck of each of his prized white horses. That morning he allowed no one else, not even his driver, Metiscus, to harness them, though the grooms fussed around with buckles and brushes and nervous advice.

Turnus himself was clad in shimmering gold, his helmet crested with scarlet. His shield hung ready. As he climbed into the chariot, he lifted his spear and ordered it loudly to tear open the cowardly heart of Aeneas. People hurried up to wish him well, but backed away in alarm when they saw his flushed cheeks and narrowed, glittering eyes.

At the edge of the Trojan camp Aeneas was speaking earnestly to his son. A small group of officers, his lifelong friends, stood by in silence. On his splendid shield each carved scene shone with promise for the future.

When the trumpet sounded from within the city, he motioned Iulus into the chariot, and stepped in after him. At his word of command the driver gathered the reins, and the chariot rolled slowly forward to the field of combat.

The thousands of Latins and Trojans and their numerous allies who thronged the plain and the walls were not the only spectators. On a nearby hilltop stood the goddess Juno, aching with bitter anxiety. A nymph stood beside her, a beautiful goddess of rivers and lakes. Her name was Juturna, half-sister to Turnus. Her eyes trickled with tears as she listened to Juno: "I have done all I can, but the Fates are too strong for me. This must be the day of your brother's defeat. If there is anything at all you can do, to put off the moment of doom, then do it!"

A magnificent procession was moving on to the arena. In a four-horse chariot King Latinus was driven to the field. His twelve-pointed crown spread a halo of light like the blaze of the rising sun. Behind him rode Turnus, his red crest shaking defiance. A retinue of attendants and priests in ceremonial robes brought cups and incense and beasts for the offerings.

From the Trojan side, a single chariot came into view. In it rode Aeneas, wearing the armour of Vulcan, and his son Ascanius, now a handsome, well-grown youth.

To the cheers and applause of their people, the chariots circled the field, and came to a stop by the holy altars. Latinus dismounted first, and held out his arms. The rivals approached him on either side, and together they faced the altars. The priests slaughtered the victims, a pig and a woolly sheep. As the smoke rose high from the roasting carcases, Aeneas drew his sword and addressed the gods:

"I call the Sun and the Earth to witness my oath. If Turnus is fortunate in this battle, and kills me with his own hand, then my son will give up his claim to this land, and the Trojans will never again make war on the Latins. But if — as I believe will happen, by the will of the gods — if my sword is victorious, and Turnus falls, I make this solemn promise. I will not enslave the people of Latium, but join the Trojan race to theirs, as equal dwellers in this land. Lavinia shall be my honoured wife, and I shall name my new city 'Lavinium' after her. I pray to the immortal gods to bless me in this venture, to you, mighty Jupiter, to Mars, the patron of warriors, and to Juno, great queen of heaven, whose goodwill I crave."

Old King Latinus stretched out a trembling hand: "I add my oath, Aeneas, by the Earth, the Sea, the Stars, by the twins Apollo and Diana, by Janus who looks both ways, and the terrible powers of Pluto. Never, never shall this pledge be broken. There will be peace between the Trojans and the Latins, whatever the outcome of this battle. May Jupiter witness these words I speak before these altars."

Now all eyes were on Turnus. The Latins craned their necks to catch his words, but they were mumbled and inaudible. The spectators looked at each other uneasily. Where were the usual ringing tones of Turnus, the fearless roar that would echo across the din of battle? Muttering grew amongst the crowd, especially in the ranks of the Rutulians: "What's the matter with him? Why doesn't he speak his prayer out loud? It looks like a bad omen to me!"

No one noticed the extra soldier in Rutulian dress. The nymph Juturna was taking advantage of the restless mood among the troops. "It's all very fine for Turnus – if he wins, he wins," she said loudly. "If he gets killed, he's a hero. But what about us? No one asked us if we want to share our land with the Trojans. We could wipe them out right now, if we take them by surprise!"

The resentment caught. Up and down the lines the Latins were arguing that the moment had come to strike, that Aeneas could not be trusted to keep the oath he had sworn, that Turnus was doomed by the gods.

And then, as the murmuring was about to break into angry clamour, an astonishing sight appeared. Across the sky, squawking loudly, a flock of wild swans flapped their wings in terrified flight. After them swooped an enormous eagle. Its power and speed were too much for the swans; exhausted, they made for the river, but as they clustered helpless on the water, the eagle seized one of them in its talons, and bore it triumphantly into the air. That should have ended the incident, but no — as if moved by a secret signal, the whole flock rose as one body and went for the eagle. Slowed down by its burden, the eagle swerved to escape, but was battered and pecked in mid-air by the furious swans. For a moment the spectators were blinded by an explosion of feathers; then, as it cleared, they saw the bedraggled eagle drop its victim and fly away. The victorious swans returned to the river.

At once a voice cried out from the Latin ranks, "What are we waiting for? Are we no better than the birds, to leave our prince to die when we have the numbers to save him? Strike now!" A spear, cast by a powerful arm, whistled across the arena. An Arcadian soldier screamed, and fell to the ground.

It was enough. A moment later the field was a blizzard of spears and hacking swords. King Latinus fled to the sidelines in terror, clutching the images of the gods. Charging horses kicked the altars aside. Men grabbed the sacred firebrands and hurled them at their enemies.

In the centre of the riot, like a rock in a raging sea, Aeneas stood bare-headed. His sword was at his side, undrawn, and he held up his open hand and shouted with all his might, "Stop this madness! The treaty is made — no one may fight except Turnus and me! Do not defy the . . ." His speech was drowned.

From somewhere an arrow flashed, and gored Aeneas deep in the thigh. He staggered with pain, and groped for support. A Trojan ran up, and helped him from the field.

"Aeneas is down!" The cry flew over the battlefield. The Trojans shuddered; the Latins cheered and attacked with added force.

When Turnus heard that Aeneas was seriously wounded, his hopes revived in an instant. The gods, it seemed, had not deserted him yet. He leapt into his chariot, and, in his wild excitement, snatched up the sword of his driver Metiscus instead of his own. With a yell of triumph, he raced into the thick of the fight. At the sight of his dazzling figure, the Trojans ran. He only laughed, and ploughed straight through with his murderous wheels. Not a man in his path escaped alive; those not trampled to death by the thundering hooves felt the bite of his spear. His chariot was splattered with enemy blood. So Turnus, drunk with the pleasure of killing, dashed over the field, and laughed.

Sick with pain, Aeneas lay gasping in the stalwart arms of Achates. The deadly barb jutted from his flesh.

"What should we do?" Iulus asked in a frightened whisper.

"Pull out the barb," Aeneas said faintly. His own fingers found the broken arrow-shaft, and he tugged once and again, till his eyes were rolling and his lips were white. The arrow had not budged.

Iapyx, the doctor, hurried up with his bag of tools and medicines, the hem of his long gown tucked into his belt: "Lie back, sir, and let me see. A nasty angle, but we'll get it out, have no fear."

He pressed the swelling skin, and tweaked the barb with a pair of forceps. Aeneas struggled in Achates' arms; he did not cry out, but his breath was grating strangely in his throat. "He'll die from the pain," an officer muttered. Iulus, huddled on the ground, was shivering.

Iapyx had set out several jars, and was deftly mixing a different potion in each. As he applied the first concoction to soothe the wound, the battle-cry of Turnus rang out, alarmingly close. The shouting and drumming of hooves grew louder and nearer. The doctor, bent on his work, ignored the noise and the billowing dust, but the others were stiff with fear. Aeneas was flinching at every touch, and the arrowhead still stuck in his flesh.

No one could see the goddess Venus as she knelt by her son and slipped a magic herb into the last of the doctor's jars. As soon as Iapyx dipped his lint in that final potion, and rubbed it gently around the wound, the swelling subsided, and Aeneas opened his eyes. "Is it out?" he said in his normal voice. Iapyx looked at his face, and took hold of the barb. It slid easily out of the wound.

Aeneas jumped up, impatiently allowed his thigh to be bandaged, and praised the doctor's skill. "It's not my doing, sir. You must thank the gods," Iapyx answered humbly. "They still have work for you to do."

In a moment Aeneas was fully armed. As he slung on his shield, he spoke briefly and quietly to Iulus: "I'll try to show you the meaning of courage. When you are a man, remember the deeds of your father Aeneas and your mighty uncle, Hector."

When the Latins saw Aeneas and heard his terrible war-cry, they forgot their recent boldness and fled in a hectic stampede. Like a blinding gale of destruction, the Trojans charged. The shrieks of dying Latins were smothered in whirling dust.

Aeneas alone took no part in the killing. The only man he wanted was Turnus. He skirted the field; he weaved in and out of the struggling fighters; he called "Turnus!" until his throat was hoarse.

Alarmed for her brother, the nymph Juturna took a flying leap into Turnus' chariot. Pushing Metiscus on to the ground, she seized the reins herself and whipped up the horses. Her figure and voice became those of the driver; Turnus never noticed the change. Over the field darted the chariot. Aeneas caught a glimpse of his speeding enemy, but before he could run down the horses and force them to stop, they had dodged out of sight. The arrogant figure of Turnus shot through the crowd in a glittering blur; with no thought of the danger around him, Aeneas dashed in pursuit.

Messapus was watching the Trojan leader. Taking careful aim, he flung his spear at close range. Aeneas ducked instantly, raising his shield. The spear screeched over his head and ripped the crest from his helmet.

Up to this point Aeneas had not dealt a single blow. Now his blood was up. Calling the gods to witness that his hand had not broken the treaty, he hurled himself into the storm.

Back and forth through the crowd rode Turnus in splendour, scattering men and weapons in all directions. He would jump down and stab with his flashing spear, whip off a man's head, helmet and all, and board the returning chariot, waving his prize.

Aeneas, no less, was hacking a path through the uproar. Powerful warriors crashed to the ground in a blood-spattered mess around him. One man he pierced through the brain, another under the ribs; three others were pinned together by his plunging spear. The treaty might never have been.

Through all the havoc on the field of battle, the walls of the city had been free from attack. They were lined with anxious citizens, peering down at the slaughter below. As Aeneas looked up, his mother Venus slipped an idea into his mind. "Prepare to storm the city!" he said to Mnestheus. "Pass the order along! I'm not waiting for Turnus to pluck up the courage to face me. The Latins broke the treaty — they can pay for it with fire!"

The order was quickly obeyed. A disciplined party of Trojan troops, armed with flaming torches, wedged themselves against the gates and the walls. Scaling-ladders were rushed from the camp.

"Latinus!" Aeneas bellowed from the surging line of attackers. "Your people broke the treaty! When your city crumbles to ash, remember the words of your solemn oath!"

Commotion broke out on the walls and down in the streets. There were many who agreed with Aeneas, and wanted the gates to be opened at once to the Trojans.

"If we let them in now, they'll spare the city!"

"Never! We'll fight to the death!" cried the others, and ran to fetch weapons.

While the citizens argued and the Trojans hammered at the gates, a shocked Queen Amata was looking out from the high palace window. She had heard for some time the din of distant battle, but now she saw blazing missiles leaping the city walls. The steady crash of a battering-ram sent tremors through the massive foundations. Amata felt the rocking and shaking within her brain; the roof seemed about to collapse; she sensed the enemy beating at her door.

"Turnus!" she cried in despair. "We need you here!" A neighbouring oil-store roared into flame. "My fault!" moaned the queen. "Turnus is dead, and the city is lost. I defied the will of the gods, and forced this war on the king!"

In his empty hall, King Latinus sat wrapped in dusty robes, calling on the gods to spare his city from ruin.

Somewhere in the palace a woman screamed. There were shouts, and running footsteps. Slowly Latinus looked up. A servant stood by the door. She began to describe what she had seen in the queen's chamber. The king understood, took hold of his robe, and tore it from neck to hem.

At the outer edge of the battlefield, Turnus, still roaring with blood-crazed laughter, was charging the Trojans with reckless courage. "Run them down!" he ordered his driver. "There are hardly any left. They've fled at the sight of my thirsty spear, the cowards!"

It was true that very few of the Trojan forces were still on the open field. Turnus, his ears ringing with the clash of steel, the thunder of hooves, and his own triumphant yells, had not noticed the commotion by the distant walls. But now he ordered the driver to stop: "What's that noise? Look there, man, the city's on fire! The Trojans are storming the gates! Quick, turn the horses!"

"No, Turnus!" the driver exclaimed. "Don't go to the city! There are plenty of people to defend the walls. Don't let these Trojans here escape alive!"

Turnus stared in astonishment. "Have your forgotten who I am?" he roared, angrily swinging the driver round by the shoulder. "Oh! Well, I might have suspected! What do you hope to gain by this trick, Juturna? You know I must fight and die. Do you want me to die a deserter, leaving my people to face Aeneas without me?"

"Sir! Turnus!" The call came from a breathless horseman, spurring an exhausted animal over the plain. "Sir, we need you!" The man was bleeding from a terrible gash on the cheek. "The Trojans are firing the city! Aeneas is battering down the gate, and the whole army is storming the walls. We can't hold them off! The city's in total panic; they say the queen has hanged herself, and the king has lost his wits!"

Gripping the chariot-rail to steady himself, Turnus gazed at the messenger and then at the city. "Well, sister," he said to Juturna, "the Fates have caught up with me. I am going to meet Aeneas at last. Please, leave me this last chance of dying with honour."

He stepped down from the chariot, and ran to the walls of the city, to the place where the fighting was thickest. "Stop! All of you, stop!" he shouted, waving his arms through the hail of arrows and spears. "Turnus is here! Let me fight, me alone, with Aeneas!"

Once again the field was quiet. The armies drew back and set down their shields. Silent crowds leaned from the walls. The ground was cleared of weapons and the mangled forms of the dead and the wounded.

With his dazzling shield at the ready, Aeneas stood poised for attack. At the other side of the clearing, Turnus, a champion in shimmering gold, gripped the earth with his toes and balanced his ten-foot spear.

At one and the same moment they launched their weapons, and ran at each other. The spears crossed in mid-air and plunged to the ground at opposite ends of the field. Sword clashed on shield. Like two mad bulls locked in desperate combat, gouging each other's flesh with their cruel horns, the rival champions closed in a furious struggle. With deadly speed the swords lunged to and fro, but every thrust met a ready shield.

Then Turnus saw his chance. Stretching to his full height, he aimed the point with terrific force at Aeneas' throat. The Trojans rose in alarm. A sudden crack — the sword, Metiscus' sword, had snapped in half. The blade was spinning away to the ground, and Turnus held only the hilt. Now, in their turn, the Latins cried out.

Turnus saw the whirling point of Aeneas' sword, and parried it — just — with his shield. He could not return the blow. Dodging from foot to foot, he knew his hopeless position, and turned to run.

In utter despair, he circled the whole arena, calling out to his friends, "Throw me a sword!"

"If you help him, I'll burn down the city!" Aeneas vowed as he raced in pursuit.

As they dashed round the field for the fifth time, Aeneas knew that he could not match Turnus in speed. The wound in his leg was throbbing and slowing him down. Glancing round for a missile, he saw his own spear, stuck in the stump of a tree at the edge of the field. With a yell of triumph, he took hold of the shaft and strained to work the head loose from the wood.

Turnus saw him and prayed, "Faunus, god of the woodland, that tree was sacred to you. The sinful Trojans cut it down to clear this battlefield. Now pity a son of your own land — hold fast to that spear."

The god must have heard, for the spear stuck firm.

While Aeneas struggled to free it, Juturna, disguised again as Metiscus, ran up to her brother and gave him his own powerful sword. As soon as she did so, Venus, invisible, helped Aeneas to pull out the spear. So they faced each other once again.

On high Olympus, the gods were watching intently. "Well, Juno," said the father of gods and men, "what more can you do? You know that Aeneas must win this battle. Why prolong the agony by sending Juturna to help her brother, when you know he is doomed? This is the end. I forbid you to do more."

Juno's reply was unusually subdued. "Very well, my lord. I give up my war with the Trojans. I have had enough of blood and death and quarrels. Let Aeneas settle in Latium, as Fate wills, and marry the Princess Lavinia. I ask only one small favour, great Jupiter."

The king of the gods smiled graciously at his penitent wife. "If it lies in my power, you may have whatever you wish."

"Let the Latin people keep their name and their ancient customs. There is no need to remember Troy in this new land. Instead of 'Trojan' (a name I can never learn to love), let their language be 'Latin', their country 'Italy', and their nation 'Rome' for all time."

"A very reasonable request," Jupiter agreed. "We'll blend the Trojan race into the Latin, and preserve the customs and traditions of this blessed land. And this, I am sure, will please you − they will faithfully worship Juno, more than any people on earth. They will be true of heart, steadfast, devoted and loyal, an inspiring example to mortals, and even to the gods."

It was time to end the duel. Jupiter kept by his throne

two hideous Furies who, on command, could swoop down to earth, spreading havoc and plague. Like the rest of their breed they had vipers for hair, and wings with the power of wind.

Down to the field of battle sped one of these creatures, with orders to drive Juturna away from her brother. In mid-flight, the Fury changed into an owl, the symbol of death, and in this sinister shape screeched loudly at Turnus and beat her wings in his face. He stiffened with fear; his limbs lost their strength, and his voice choked in his throat.

Juturna recognized Jupiter's herald of death. She could no longer help her brother. Weeping bitterly, lamenting that she could not die with Turnus, she dived in the river and vanished.

And now Aeneas, raising high his enormous spear, advanced and shouted his challenge. Turnus answered bravely, "Save your breath! Jupiter makes me tremble, not your threats!" and, heaving up a gigantic rock, a boundary-stone so big and heavy that twelve strong men could hardly move it, he charged at Aeneas.

But even as he hurled the rock, Turnus knew it was no use. His limbs seemed leaden; it was like trying to run in a nightmare. The rock crashed to the ground a yard in front of his feet. All he could see was the lowering point of the spear.

It struck. Turnus' shield, with its seven strong layers, was ripped apart; the point gored deep in his thigh. He tumbled on to his knees, and stretched out a hand in entreaty.

"Aeneas, take Lavinia for your wife. You have beaten me; everyone knows it. Only, I beg you, have pity on my father — let him have me back, alive or dead, as you desire."

Aeneas stood over him, his sword poised, but did not strike. The battle was won; he had no need for the death of Turnus. His glance ran over the humbled warrior, and a glint of metal caught his eye. It was Pallas' belt, the trophy that Turnus had stripped from the corpse of that brave young man.

"Pity? What pity did you show for Pallas, or for *his* aged father? How dare you flaunt the spoils that you took from him, and beg for pity? Now Pallas, Pallas himself, has come to strike you dead!" Seething with rage, Aeneas plunged his sword into Turnus' heart.

So Turnus died, and his spirit flew to the Land of Shades.

Epilogue   The Founding of Rome

ACCORDING to legend, Aeneas did marry Lavinia, and named his new city "Lavinium" in her honour. Three years later, after seeing his Trojans well settled in Latium, mixing freely and peacefully with the Latins, Aeneas died.

For thirty years his son ruled in Lavinium, and then, as had been foretold, founded a city of his own, called "Alba Longa". Three hundred years went by, and still the descendants of Aeneas reigned secure in Alba Longa, king after king, for twelve generations. But at last serious trouble arose in the kingdom.

When King Procas died, the throne should have passed, by custom, to his elder son, Numitor, a man with several sons and one daughter, Rhea Silvia. Numitor's brother, however, a ruthless and ambitious man called Amulius, was eager to make himself king. Gathering some followers together, Amulius forced Numitor to give up his throne and go into exile in the country.

The next step Amulius took was to murder all Numitor's sons. This left only the daughter, Rhea Silvia. Amulius was not afraid of this young girl, but he wanted to make sure that she would never marry, for if she did, her husband or sons might one day seek the throne. He thought of a foolproof plan.

165

There was in Alba a temple sacred to the goddess Vesta, whose holy flame was tended night and day by a group of dedicated priestesses. These women lived in the temple, shut away from men, and were strictly forbidden to marry. Amulius, pretending that he was doing his niece a great honour, enrolled her in this order of Vestal Virgins, and then settled down to enjoy his reign.

The gods, however, cannot be stopped so easily. Rhea Silvia was visited secretly by Mars, the god of war, who could enter the temple, despite locked doors and solid walls. They fell in love, and before long Rhea Silvia had given birth to twin boys.

Amulius was appalled by this news: "It is a disgrace for a Vestal to bear a child. The infants must be destroyed, and the sinful mother put in prison for life."

Servants were ordered to fling the double cradle into the River Tiber at once. They did so and left quickly, glad to be free of their unpleasant duty. They did not notice that the cradle floated on the stream, and soon came to rest in the reeds by the muddy riverbank.

The hungry babies cried, and a she-wolf, coming down to drink in the river, put her head in the cradle to investigate. She lifted the babies gently out and suckled them like her own cubs.

Before long a herdsman called Faustulus, who looked after the royal flocks, came upon the astonishing sight. He exclaimed in surprise, and the wolf darted away at the sound of his voice. Faustulus took the twins home to his wife, and there, in a humble cottage, the boys grew up.

Faustulus had heard rumours about Rhea Silvia and her sons, and it did not take him long to guess that his adopted children were King Amulius' grand-nephews. When the boys had grown into stalwart youths, he told them the story of their birth and their uncle's crime. "Your blood is royal," he said. "Your names are Romulus and Remus."

The young men led a simple, hardy life in the woods and fields, and with a band of friends, took to hunting game and chasing robbers and brigands, whose loot they seized and shared amongst themselves. In time they came to the notice of Numitor, who lived in exile not far from their haunts. Numitor, in delight, recognized the twins as his long-lost grandsons.

Together they plotted against the wicked king. With the support of their friends, they attacked the palace, captured Amulius, and put him to death. The people of Alba were not sorry to be rid of him, and welcomed Numitor back as their rightful king.

Romulus and Remus, now that their grandfather was restored to the throne, soon grew tired of living as princes in the court at Alba. They decided to build a new city by the Tiber, at the very place where Evander had first greeted Aeneas and where they themselves had been rescued as babies. Many citizens of Alba were eager to follow them, for that city was already too small for its growing population.

Unfortunately both Romulus and Remus wanted to rule as king in the new city. Their rivalry grew bitter. "The gods favour me," said Remus. "I saw six vultures in the sky, coming to salute me."

"That is nothing," retorted his brother, "Twelve vultures were sent to greet me, so it is clear that the gods favour me twice as much as you. I will be king!"

"King of what?" scoffed Remus. "These city walls are so low I can jump over them!" And he leapt over the half-built foundations. Romulus lost his temper. Seizing his sword, he killed his brother Remus.

Romulus completed the new city, and named it after himself. And that was how a descendant of Aeneas came to found the city of Rome, which rose in splendour and power to be mistress of the world.

Glossary

ACESTES half-Trojan ruler of settlement in Sicily

ACHATES close friend of **Aeneas**

ACHILLES Greek hero in the **Trojan War**

AGAMEMNON ruler of **Mycenae** and chief king among the Greeks at the **Trojan War**; brother of **Menelaus**

AENEAS son of **Venus** and the Trojan **Anchises**; leader of the expedition to found a new city after the fall of Troy

AJAX one of the Greek leaders in the **Trojan War**

ALBA also called "Alba Longa", city in **Latium** to be founded one day by **Aeneas'** son

ALETES senior Trojan officer

ALLECTO one of the Furies, dreaded goddesses of revenge and bloodshed

AMATA queen of the **Laurentes**, wife of King **Latinus**

ANCHISES Trojan noble, father of **Aeneas**

ANDROMACHE wife of the Trojan hero **Hector**, captured by **Pyrrhus**, later married to **Helenus**

ANIUS king of **Delos**

ANNA sister of **Dido**

APOLLO god of prophecy, medicine, archery

ARCADIA district in Greece, original home of **Evander** and the settlers of **Pallanteum**

ARDEA   town in **Latium** in Italy, centre of the **Rutulians**, home of **Turnus**

ARRUNS   Etruscan soldier, slayer of **Camilla**

ASCANIUS   son of **Aeneas**, also called **Iulus**

ATLAS   giant of divine race, supporter of the sky

AUGUSTUS   see **Caesar Augustus**

AVENTINUS   son of **Hercules**, ally of **Turnus**

BACCHUS   god of wine, worshipped with hysterical singing and dancing

BEROE   Trojan lady in **Aeneas'** party

BITIAS   Trojan soldier, brother of **Pandarus**

BRUTUS   first elected leader (consul) in **Rome**, 509 B.C.

CACUS   fire-breathing ogre killed by **Hercules**

CAECULUS   leader of one of the armies allied with **Turnus**

CAESAR AUGUSTUS   63 B.C.–A.D. 14, great-nephew of **Julius Caesar**, known as the first emperor of Rome; the **Aeneid** was written to please him

CAESAR (JULIUS)   Roman general who won great power (102–44 B.C.)

CALCHAS   priest and prophet attached to the Greek army in the **Trojan War**

CAMILLA   maiden warrior, ally of **Turnus**, and leader of the **Volscians**

CAPITOL   citadel of **Rome**, containing the great temple of **Jupiter Best and Greatest**

CARTHAGE   city in North Africa, founded by **Dido**; in historical times, an enemy of Rome

CASSANDRA   daughter of **Priam**, who uttered true warnings which no one ever believed

CATO   known as the "Censor", Roman famous for conservative views and undying patriotism, 232–147 B.C.

CERBERUS   three-headed watchdog in the Underworld, once captured by **Hercules**

CERES   goddess of crops

CHARON   ferryman on the River **Styx** in the Underworld

CHARYBDIS   dangerous whirlpool on Sicilian side of the Straits of Messina

CLAUSUS   an ally of **Turnus**

CLEOPATRA   queen of Egypt, loved by **Mark Antony**; defeated in 31 B.C. by Octavian, later called **Caesar Augustus**

CLOANTHUS   a Trojan in **Aeneas'** party

COROEBUS   young man engaged to **Cassandra**

CREUSA   wife of **Aeneas**, mother of **Ascanius**

CUPID   son of **Venus**, boy-god who makes people fall in love

CYCLOPS   (plural: Cyclopes) one-eyed giant

DARDANUS   an ancestor of the Trojan race, born in Italy

DARES   a Trojan boxer

DEIPHOBUS   son of **Priam**, married **Helen** after the death of **Paris**

DELOS   island in the Aegean Sea, sacred to **Apollo**

DIANA   maiden-goddess of hunting and the moon

DIDO   queen of **Carthage**

DIOMEDES   Greek warrior who fought at **Troy**, considered almost as mighty as **Achilles**

DRANCES   a councillor among the **Laurentes** and a personal enemy of **Turnus**

ELYSIUM   part of the Underworld reserved for noble souls, a happy, beautiful place, also called the Elysian Fields

ENTELLUS   champion boxer from Sicily

ETRUSCANS   race of people living in Italy; from them the Romans derived many ideas, including the alphabet and divination

EURYALUS   young Trojan, friend of **Nisus**

EVANDER   Greek king from **Arcadia**, ruler of **Pallanteum**, ally of **Aeneas** and father of **Pallas**

FABIUS, QUINTUS   (died 203 B.C.) emergency leader ("dictator") appointed in Rome to defend it against Hannibal of **Carthage**. He did not attack, but preferred to wear the enemy down slowly. He was thus called "Cunctator", meaning "Delayer"

FATE   mysterious power, stronger than the gods, which decides future events. Sometimes personified as three goddesses called "The Fates"

GAULS   natives of country now known as France

GRACCHUS   two brothers, Tiberius (died 132 B.C.) and Gaius (died 122 B.C.) who tried to bring in social reforms in Rome

GYAS   a Trojan in **Aeneas'** party

HALAESUS   son of **Agamemnon**, an ally of **Turnus**

HARPIES   dreadful bird-women, living in the **Strophades**

HECATE   goddess of black magic

HECTOR   eldest son of King **Priam** of **Troy**; best Trojan fighter, killed by **Achilles**

HECUBA   queen of **Troy**, wife of **Priam**

HELEN   most beautiful woman in the world, wife of the Greek **Menelaus**; she eloped to **Troy** with **Paris**, thus causing the **Trojan War**

HELENUS   son of **Priam**, a priest with powers of prophecy

HERCULES   very famous hero, son of **Jupiter**, known

for his strength and mighty deeds

HORATIUS   legendary Roman hero who defended his city by blocking the bridge across the **Tiber**

IAPYX   doctor in **Aeneas'** army

IARBAS   an African chieftain, disappointed suitor of **Dido**

IDA, MOUNT   mountain near **Troy**

ILIONEUS   a Trojan officer under **Aeneas**

IRIS   servant of **Juno**, goddess of rainbows

IULUS   son of **Aeneas**, also known as **Ascanius**

JANUS   Italian god of doorways and entrances after whom "January" is named

JUNO   queen of the gods, wife of **Jupiter**

JUPITER   king of the gods, lord of the thunderbolt

JUTURNA   a water-nymph, half-sister to **Turnus**

LAOCOON   a Trojan priest who mistrusted the Wooden Horse

LATIN   race of people living in part of Italy called **Latium**

LATINUS   king of the **Laurentes**, a **Latin** tribe

LATIUM   area in central Italy, containing **Rome**

LAURENTES   **Latin** tribe whose city, ruled by **Latinus**, was the centre of power in **Latium**

LAUSUS   son of the **Etruscan** ex-tyrant **Mezentius**

LAVINIA   daughter of **Latinus** and **Amata**, later married to **Aeneas**

LETHE   river in the Underworld; its water makes the dead forget their past lives

MARK ANTONY   (83–31 B.C.) partner and later rival of Octavian (the earlier name of **Caesar Augustus**); lover of **Cleopatra**

MARS   god of war

MENELAUS   Greek husband of **Helen** and brother of **Agamemnon**

MERCURY   messenger of the gods

MESSAPUS   son of **Neptune** and an ally of **Turnus**

METISCUS   **Turnus'** chariot-driver

MEZENTIUS   expelled tyrant of the **Etruscans** and ally of **Turnus**

MINERVA   goddess of wisdom

MISENUS   a Trojan warrior

MNESTHEUS   a Trojan officer under **Aeneas**

MOTHER, GREAT   goddess of earth; regarded as mother of all gods and men, worshipped especially in Crete and the East

MYCENAE   city in Greece, home of **Agamemnon**

NAUTES   veteran officer in **Aeneas'** party

NEPTUNE   god of the sea, brother of **Jupiter**

NISUS   Trojan warrior, friend of **Euryalus**

NUMANUS   a **Latin** warrior, brother-in-law to **Turnus**

OEBALUS   an ally of **Turnus**

OLYMPUS   high mountain in northern Greece, believed to be the home of the gods

OPIS   nymph attendant of the goddess **Diana**

ORESTES   son of **Agamemnon**

ORPHEUS   famous musician who persuaded **Pluto** to let him fetch his wife Eurydice from the Underworld

PALAMEDES   one of the leading Greeks in the **Trojan War**

PALINURUS   steersman of **Aeneas'** ship

PALLANTEUM   Greek settlement in **Latium**, ruled by **Evander**

PALLAS   son of **Evander** and squire of **Aeneas** in battle

PANDARUS   a Trojan soldier, brother of **Bitias**

PANTHUS   a Trojan

PARIS   son of **Priam** of **Troy**, eloped with **Helen**

PLUTO   (also called Hades or Dis) god of the Under-world, brother of **Jupiter**

POLITES   youngest son of **Priam**

POLYDORUS   son of **Priam**, killed in **Thrace**

POMPEY   (106–48 B.C.) political rival of **Julius Caesar**, defeated by him after civil war in Italy

PRIAM   king of **Troy**, husband of **Hecuba**, father of **Hector**, **Paris**, **Deiphobus**, **Polydorus**, **Polites**, **Helenus** and **Cassandra**

PROSERPINA   wife of **Pluto**, queen of the Underworld

PYGMALION   cruel brother of **Dido** and ruler in **Tyre**

PYRRHUS   son of **Achilles** and killer of **Priam**

REMUS   twin brother of **Romulus**

ROME   powerful city on the River **Tiber** in Italy, said to be founded in 753 B.C. by **Romulus**; centre of the greatest empire in the ancient world

ROMULUS   descendant of **Aeneas**, founder of **Rome**

RUTULIANS   **Latin** tribes, led by **Turnus**

SABINES   Italian tribe, later absorbed into the population of **Rome**

SALIUS   a Trojan in **Aeneas'** party

SATURN   Italian god, in legend the father of **Jupiter**, said to be the earliest ruler of Italy

SCYLLA   six-headed monster, believed to live on the Italian side of the Straits of Messina

SERGESTUS   a Trojan in **Aeneas'** party

SCIPIO   famous Roman family. One of them (Scipio Africanus Major) defeated the Carthaginian Hannibal in 201 B.C.

SIBYL   strange priestess of **Apollo** living in Cumae in western Italy

SILVIA   **Latin** village girl, owner of stag wounded by **Iulus**

SILVIUS   son of **Aeneas** and **Lavinia**

SINON   Greek who posed as a deserter in order to deceive the Trojans and persuade them to take the Wooden Horse into their city

STROPHADES   islands in the Ionian Sea, home of the **Harpies**

STYX   river in the Underworld, across which only the buried dead may pass

SYCHAEUS   husband of **Dido**, murdered by **Pygmalion**

TARCHON   king of the **Etruscans**, ally of **Aeneas**

TARQUINS   family of **Etruscan** rulers of **Rome**. The last one, an unpopular tyrant called Tarquin the Proud, was driven out of **Rome** in 510 B.C.

TARTARUS   part of the Underworld where the wicked are punished

TEUCER   an ancestor of the Trojan race

THESEUS   legendary Greek hero, descended from **Neptune**, who once tried to abduct **Proserpina** from the Underworld

THRACE   area N.E. of Greece, roughly modern Bulgaria

TIBER   river on which **Rome** is built

TROJAN WAR   fought by the Greeks against the city of **Troy** to try to recover **Helen**; lasted ten years and ended with the destruction of **Troy**

TROY   rich and powerful city in Asia Minor

TURNUS   chieftain of a Latin tribe called **Rutulians**;

suitor of **Lavinia**, enemy of **Aeneas**

TYRE   seaport in Phoenicia (now Lebanon), original home of **Dido**

ULYSSES   one of the leading Greeks at the **Trojan War**, noted for his cunning wiles (also called "Odysseus")

UMBRO   an ally of **Turnus**

VENUS   goddess of love and beauty, mother of **Aeneas**

VIRBIUS   an ally of **Turnus**

VOLSCIANS   an Italian race, allied with **Turnus**, led by **Camilla**

VULCAN   god of craftsmanship and fire, husband of **Venus**